Black and Reformed

Allan Boesak

Black and Reformed

Apartheid, Liberation, and the Calvinist Tradition

Edited by Leonard Sweetman

Maryknoll, New York 10545

The Catholic Foreign Mission Society of America (Maryknoll) recruits and trains people for overseas missionary service. Through Orbis Books Maryknoll aims to foster the international dialogue that is essential to mission. The books published, however, reflect the opinions of their authors and are not meant to represent the official position of the society.

Manufactured in the United States of America
Published in 1984 by Orbis Books, Maryknoll, NY 10545

Manuscript Editor: William E. Jerman

Library of Congress Cataloging in Publication Data

Boesak, Allan Aubrey, 1946-
Black and reformed.

Includes bibliographical references.
1. South Africa—Race relations—Addresses, essays, lectures. 2. Race relations—religious aspects—Reformed Church—Addresses, essays, lectures.
3. Reformed Church—Doctrines—Addresses, essays, lectures. 4. Black theology—Addresses, essays, lectures. I. Title.
DT763.B55 1984 261.8′348′00968 84-7212
ISBN 0-88344-148-9 (pbk.)

For Desmond Tutu
Prophet of God
Shepherd of his people
Brother and Friend
in whom God's gifts
are seen and admired

Contents

Foreword xi
Acknowledgments xvii

Chapter 1
The Courage to Be Black:
Black Theology and the Struggle for Liberation 1
The Judge says "Terrible!" 1
You Have Seen . . . God's Righteousness and Human Rights 6
The Black Messiah and Black Humanity 10
Black Theology, Black Identity, and the Future 15

Chapter 2
The Black Church and the Future 20
The Struggle of the Black Church 22
Reconciliation and Confrontation 29

Chapter 3
Divine Obedience:
A Letter to the Minister of Justice 32

Chapter 4
Wholeness through Liberation 42
Systemic Violence 43
Where Is the Church? 47

Chapter 5
Guarding the Faith: Reflections on the Banning of Black Theology Literature in South Africa 52
"Guardian of the Faith"? 53
Imagine, God Forbid . . . 60

Chapter 6
Holding on to the Vision **62**

Chapter 7
Liberation and the Churches of Africa:
"To Break Every Yoke" **70**
The God of the Bible *71*
False Gods and Their Idols *77*

Chapter 8
You Are a True Son of South Africa:
An Open Letter to Bishop Desmond Tutu **79**
Response *82*

Chapter 9
Black and Reformed:
Contradiction or Challenge? **83**
Apartheid: Heritage of the Reformed Tradition *84*
Exigencies of a Black, Reformed Future *94*

Chapter 10
God Made Us All, But . . .
Racism and the World Alliance of Reformed Churches **100**
Racism: Structured Sinfulness *102*
Challenge to the World Alliance of Reformed Churches *108*

Chapter 11
The Present Crisis in Apartheid:
A Reply to the South African Government Proposal for a Three-Tier Parliament **111**
The New Constitutional Proposals *112*
Two Versions of Basically the Same Policy *118*

Chapter 12
Apartheid after the WARC Decisions in Ottawa, 1982 **123**
A Long History *124*
Apartheid Intensified *128*

Chapter 13
“Where Is Your Brother . . . ?” (Genesis 4:9) **137**

Chapter 14
Jesus Christ, the Life of the World **146**

Chapter 15
Peace in Our Day **155**

Notes **165**

Foreword

With two exceptions—the letter to Minister of Justice Alwyn Schlebusch (chapter 3) and the letter to Bishop Desmond Tutu (chapter 8)—this work represents a collection of addresses that Allan Aubrey Boesak delivered between 1974 and 1983 to assemblies of Christian believers, church representatives, ecclesiastical administrators, college and university students, and (chapter 15) to black citizens of South Africa as they were organizing themselves into a political movement. Although the addresses were delivered over the span of a decade on three continents, they reflect always the continuing experience of South African blacks, long oppressed by South African whites. Never does Allan Boesak leave this theme. When he delivers an address, the voice may be that of Allan Boesak, but the pulse is that of South Africa's suffering black people.

In these addresses South African blacks do not constitute an undifferentiated mass, an amorphous entity. Specific black people emerge concretely in the framework of their suffering. The reader meets the mother of Bernard Fortuin; the police prevented her from ministering to her son as he was lying in the street, dying from a police officer's bullet. The reader meets an older, unnamed woman in an illegal housing settlement; she is left at the mercy of the inclement weather when a police officer, during a raid on the settlement to destroy the homes there, snatched from her the piece of plastic she had salvaged from the wreckage to try to protect herself from the wind and rain. And the reader meets unnamed students, young people and children who stood up to police intimidation as they protested the injustice of an educational system whose inequities guarantee that blacks will not compete on a par with whites in the job market and in society. Allan

Boesak's voice is the voice of these suffering blacks. In these addresses the suffering black people cry out to the peoples of the world and to God for liberation from their oppression:

> How long must I bear pain in my soul,
> and have sorrow in my heart all the day? [Psalm 13:2]

The individual suffering blacks whom one meets in Allan Boesak's addresses do not provide an anecdotal dimension to the addresses. If one assumes that the blacks he introduces serve this role, then one overlooks the essential character of these addresses—their theological character. If one takes seriously, however, the role of these addresses, serving as the voice of South African blacks as they cry out for deliverance, for liberation, then one can recognize that these addresses represent what Kosuke Koyama calls a "theology from below," theology that emerges from the everyday experience of people where they truly are, from the marketplace of life.

In these addresses, moreover, one can discern quickly that Allan Boesak does not mediate the experience of South African blacks in isolation from the word of God. The black experience functions as a vehicle enabling them to hear the word of God in a way in which they may not have heard it before. In their context they hear the word of God as that which brings freedom to those in bondage, deliverance to those under oppression, light to those who stumble in darkness, life to those who subsist in the midst of death, and good news to those who live in poverty. The word of God, as the black South Africans hear it in their context, in turn, casts light upon the situation in which they live in South Africa. It enables South African blacks to cope with their situation and equips them to persist in their pursuit of true and full humanity. Nowhere does this "theology from below" function more clearly than in chapter 13, the sermon entitled "Where Is Your Brother?" In this sermon the circumstances in which blacks live in South Africa enable them to hear the story of Cain and Abel, the story of the first fratricide, with a meaning they had never discerned before, a meaning that may surprise whites in North America, Europe, and South Africa. The story of Cain and Abel,

heard in this way, illumines the situation in which blacks find themselves in South Africa with the result that it aids them to cope with life so they can take the next step in their struggle to achieve authentic humanity.

His use of "theology from below" does not mean that Allan Boesak dissociates himself from the historical church, that his position is discontinuous with the Christian tradition. Nor does it mean that he is ignorant of the classic theological systems that church reformers elaborated in the sixteenth century. In fact, he chose the title for this collection of addresses: *Black and Reformed.* The title comes from the charter of the Alliance of Black Reformed Christians in Southern Africa, written in 1981—a charter in which black Christians deliberately attempt to rescue the Reformed perspective from the deviation from or distortion of that tradition characteristic of the teaching and practice of the white Afrikaner Reformed churches in South Africa. In this title Allan Boesak wishes to identify himself with the sixteenth-century efforts to institute reforms in the church designed to bring it, in faith and life, into subjection to and conformity with the Word of God. Specifically, he wishes to identify himself with the reformation movement associated with John Calvin in Geneva.

Why does Allan Boesak wish to identify himself with the reformation movement associated with John Calvin in Geneva? The Nederduits Gereformeerde Kerk and the Nederduits Hervormde Kerk associate themselves with the same roots. These white Afrikaner Reformed churches, moreover, claim to represent and continue the faithful development of the sixteenth-century Genevan reformation. These white Afrikaner Reformed churches, however, spawned the apartheid or "separate development" model of society that dehumanizes all black people in South Africa.

In 1881 the Nederduits Gereformeerde Kerk gave birth to the Nederduits Gereformeerde Zendingkerk, or Mission Church, of which Allan Boesak is a member and minister. Chris Loff, a Mission Church pastor and theologian, describes this event as the "final solution" to the "problem."[1] In establishing the Mission Church, the Nederduits Gereformeerde Kerk institutionalized the separate assemblies of blacks and whites for worship and the Eucharist, which, in 1857, had originated as a temporary pragmatic solution to the "problems" generated in the church because of the "weakness of some" white Reformed Christians. In the light of this background, how can Allan Boesak, the voice of suffering blacks in South Africa, advertise the position *Black and Reformed?* How can this position enhance the struggle of black people in South Africa to gain true humanity?

With some frequency Allan Boesak points out that he discovered significant differences between the Reformed tradition transmitted to the blacks of South Africa by the white Afrikaner Reformed churches and the teaching he found in the writings of Calvin. These differences are most significant in the areas of the relationship between the Christian citizen and the magistrate, of the interpersonal relationships among all Christians, and of the use of "the present life and its helps." The white Afrikaner Reformed churches transmitted a version of their tradition that had developed in the context of the relationships between blacks and whites in South Africa. It provided the white Afrikaner Reformed churches with what, in their judgment, was a Christian warrant for the "separate development" model of society.

Allan Boesak is among the younger theologians in the black Reformed churches who recognize the necessity of their Christian antecedents in order to demonstrate that their struggle for true humanity today is not disobedience to the word of God. This struggle, rather, is one engaged in by men and women and children who seek, in continuity with those involved in the sixteenth-century Genevan reformation, to live a response of praise and adoration of, and obedience and service to, the Lord whose lordship is exercised over every square inch of the creation.

In concert with his peers in the Alliance of Black Reformed Christians in Southern Africa, Allan Boesak commits himself "to come to a truer understanding of the Reformed tradition and accept the challenge to articulate [his] faith in terms that are authentic and relevant." He and his peers "begin doing so by declaring unequivocally that apartheid is a sin and that the moral and theological justification of it is a travesty of the gospel, a betrayal of the Reformed tradition, and a heresy." He and his peers confess that they "take courage and comfort in life and in death from the assurance, given [them] by the Belgic Confession, that 'the faithful and elect shall be crowned with glory and honour; and the Son of God will confess their name before God and his father. . . . All tears shall be wiped from their eyes; *and their cause which is now condemned by many judges and magistrates as heretical and impious will then be known to be the cause of the Son of God.' "* Allan Boesak and his peers conclude this charter with the assertion: "This is our tradition. This we will fight for."[2]

These young theologians are the voice of large numbers in the black Reformed churches in South Africa. They wish to return to what they recognize as the vital and creative source of their tradition. They assert that they stand in a relationship of real and true continuity with this tradition; that they stand in direct continuity, therefore, with the authentic Christian tradition. In this framework Allan Boesak exercises his role: a voice of those who are black and Reformed.

LEONARD SWEETMAN

Notes

1. Chris Loff, "The History of a Heresy," in John W. de Gruchy and Charles Villa-Vicencio, eds., *Apartheid Is a Heresy* (Grand Rapids: William B. Eerdmans, 1983), p. 22.

2. "The Charter of the Alliance of Black Reformed Christians in Southern Africa," *Apartheid Is a Heresy,* p. 165. This Charter was adopted by the Alliance (ABRECSA) at its first conference, which convened at Hammanskraal, South Africa, October 26–30, 1981. The complete text of the Charter is found in *Apartheid Is a Heresy,* pp. 161–68.

Acknowledgments

Since the academic year 1980–1981, when Allan Aubrey Boesak served as the guest lecturer in the Multicultural Lectureship Program at Calvin College in Grand Rapids, Michigan, he and I have collaborated in sifting through his addresses, sermons, and class lectures for the purpose of producing a collection which reflects well the way in which the evangel sounds clearly and consistently in all that he does. Now that this project is completed, I must express my thanks to all those who have made the project possible. Working closely with Allan Boesak has been a religious experience. I appreciate his deep piety and his insistence upon using effectively the tradition he has inherited in the Christian community as a resource adequate to the task of calling all his compatriots, black and white, to obedient service to Jesus the Lord.

I wish to thank the publishers who hold the rights to essays which appear in this collection and who graciously have given permission to publish those materials:

J. H. Kok, Kampen, The Netherlands, for "The Courage to Be Black," Chapter 1. The essay first appeared in *Wereld en zending* 3 (1974) 265–85. In a slightly different form it was also included in *Om het zwart te zeggen. Een bundel opstellen over centrale thema's in de zwarte theologie,* Allan Boesak, ed. (Kampen: J. H. Kok, 1975), pp. 12–28.

The World Council of Churches' for "The Black Church and the Future," Chapter 2, which appeared as "The Black Church and the Struggle in South Africa" in *The Ecumenical Review* 32 (1980) 16–24, and for "Holding on to the Vision," Chapter 6, which appeared in a slightly different form in *One World* 69 (Aug.-Sept. 1981) 19–20.

Church and Society (71 [1981] 31–39), for "Wholeness through Liberation," Chapter 4. This address was also given to the Social Welfare Ministries Conference sponsored by the Presbyterian Health, Education, and Welfare Association, Louisville, Kentucky, Feb. 4–8, 1981.

Theology Today (38 [1981–82], pp. 182–89), for "Guarding the Faith," Chapter 5.

The Remonstrant Brotherhood in Utrecht, The Netherlands, for "Apartheid after the WARC Decisions in Ottawa, 1982," Chapter 12, and "Where Is Your Brother . . .?", Chapter 13.

The William B. Eerdmans Publishing Company, for "Black and Reformed: Contradiction or Challenge?", Chapter 9, which appeared in *The Reformed Journal* 31 (1981) 13–18; "God Made Us All, But . . . ," Chapter 10, which appeared in *Apartheid Is a Heresy,* edited by John W. de Gruchy and Charles Villa-Vicencio; and "Jesus Christ, the Life of the World," Chapter 14, which appeared in *Gathered For Life,* edited by David Gill, the official report of the sixth assembly of the World Council of Churches, Vancouver, Canada, 1983. The World Council of Churches published this report in Geneva and has also granted permission to use this essay.

Allan Boesak provided his own translation of "Divine Obedience: A Letter to the Minister of Justice," Chapter 3; and Leonard Sweetman translated "The Courage to Be Black," Chapter 1, "Apartheid after the WARC Decisions in Ottawa, 1982," Chapter 12, and "Where Is Your Brother?", Chapter 13.

My special thanks are due to Beverly Luchies Stephenson, who during the summer of 1981 meticulously transcribed cassettes which contained Allan Boesak's addresses, sermons, and class lectures. I am deeply grateful, also, to Donna Quist and Esther Vander Tuig, the secretaries of the Religion and Theology Department at Calvin College, who went far beyond the call of duty as they patiently and carefully typed the manuscript of these essays. Also, I thank the administration of Calvin College for providing me a leave during January 1984, for the purpose of completing this manuscript. Finally, I thank John Eagleson of Orbis Books for guiding me through this project with his kind and courteous demeanor. This has proven to be a big asset from November 1980, when I first had a conversation with him about this project.

LEONARD SWEETMAN
Calvin College,
Grand Rapids, Michigan

Chapter I

The Courage to Be Black: Black Theology and the Struggle for Liberation

The Judge Says "Terrible!"

This is the headline over a story that appeared in the Sunday edition of a South African newspaper. The paper reported that three white men captured an 11-year-old black boy when he attempted to steal a few pieces of coal from the South African Railroads. As punishment they stripped him and forced him to sit down on the hot boiler of their steam locomotive. Four weeks after the incident a doctor who examined the boy's buttocks described the burns in terms of "the most severe degree." The judge characterized the entire incident as "terrible" and "extremely bad." He sentenced each of the men to a punishment of six lashes and three years in prison. He then suspended the prison sentences.

This incredible incident is the sort of act one associates with the Ku Klux Klan of old. But it did not happen very long ago. The report appeared in the newspaper *Rapport* on December 16, 1973.

Now let us look at another example. Black women who, be-

This essay first appeared in *Wereld en zending* (the Netherlands), 3 (1974) 265–85. The text has been edited for inclusion in the present collection.

cause of poverty and unemployment, are not able to survive in the "native homelands" (Bantustans) are forced to go to the "white" cities for employment. In addition to their employment contract, in Johannesburg they must sign another contract: their children will never come to live with them. A visit from the children, even during a vacation period, can cost the mother her job. This report is found in *The Star*, September 18, 1973.

In another story, a special worship service was held in Upington in the Northwest Cape. In this service the congregation prayed that the government would abandon its plan to uproot 920 persons who live in the village of Riemvasmaak and force them to settle in a newly opened area in Damaraland, Namibia, 1,300 kilometers (800 miles) away from their old home. Appeals, tears, and prayers were to no avail. The villagers, according to a newspaper report, were to be forced, in January 1974, to leave the land where they had lived more than sixty years. The magistrate empowered as "the Bantu" for the Kakamas area, Mr. G. J. J. Jordaan, according to the newspaper report, said that "the majority were happy" and were "prepared to move."[1]

These stories are not isolated cases. South African blacks know this very well. They know also that such reports do not tell even half the story. Such facts, horrible as they are, constitute the daily experience of dehumanization that is structured into the system of apartheid. They shape the total black experience. Along with the effects of countless other laws, these laws constitute part of what are said to be necessary elements in "Western Christian civilization": necessary, that is, for white security and white survival. They are said to be part of "nonwhite self-determination." They are said to be signposts that point to real racial peace. They are, however, more than this.

If we are to believe white pastors, all of this humiliation and dehumanization is the declared will of God, God's holy ordinances, which human beings, specifically blacks, may not change. Whites are God's elect. They alone have the right to health, wealth, education, and humanity. They may designate their status as God-given, though it may be an idolatrous status. As in so many other instances, whites may erect a signpost with the warning "For Whites Only" to describe and define "humanity." For blacks, obviously, there are criteria other than those involved in defining what is "human." This is the heart of the matter.

As early as 1804, and even earlier, the Dutch referred to their slaves in Surinam as "these objects."[2] In the nineteenth century, George Theal, a Cape Colony historian, wrote about the work of both the Surinamese and black African slaves:

> They did not feel that they were humiliated by forced labor. Nor did they feel humiliated by standing naked in public to be bought and sold. They were the most cheerful of all creatures. If you attempt to evaluate their situation by describing how a European would feel in these circumstances you will draw erroneous conclusions *because their upbringing and their thought patterns are totally and completely different from those of the Europeans.*[3]

Theal describes something back there, *then*, in the nineteenth century. But in 1973, in Johannesburg, hundreds of black children were taken away from their parents by the government and were sent to "homelands." By virtue of one or another of the apartheid laws, the parents, although they were married, could be regarded as unmarried. Mr. Coen Kotzè, an official of the Bantu Administration, explained this action of the government: "Black women prefer not to live with their children."[4] This happened in the here and now, in the 1970s.

You can see that the attitudes of whites toward blacks have not changed very much. Blacks, of course, have known this all along. After all, we must live with this every day! This same contempt for the humanity of blacks is visible, also, in the mere lip service that South Africa has paid to the United Nations' Universal Declaration of Human Rights. In a study by the International Commission of Jurists that appeared a few years ago, it was clearly and convincingly demonstrated that the ideology and practice of apartheid entails the violation of at least twenty articles of the UN declaration. For the sake of completeness, I shall mention the relevant acticles: 1, 2, 3, 5, 6, 7, 9, 10, 11, 12, 13, 16, 17, 18, 19, 20, 21, 23, 25, 26. A newspaper informs me that this study has been proscribed and banned in South Africa. When shall we learn that the truth cannot be banned?

It is quite evident that in South Africa blacks have no rights that whites must respect. This is evident in the name that whites give us. We are "nonwhites." Humanity is confined to "whites." "Nonwhite" points to a nonperson. "Nonwhite" is a negation. "Nonwhite" points to a nonentity with which you need not concern yourself. Blacks, quite correctly, reject the term "nonwhite" as well as the terms "colored" and "Bantu." These terms are used in the language of the oppressor. We deny that the right to a humane existence is the exclusive right of whites. We refuse any longer to be defined and limited by whites. With glowing pride in our blackness we oppose this "colonializing" of our humanity. We can no longer be sacrificed to white self-centeredness and greed. We can no longer be the victims of white alienation.

In this situation black Christians attempt to answer the questions and to discharge the obligations that confront us in the gospel. It becomes evident, of course, that we cannot content ourselves with either white questions or white answers. Our theological reflection must take into consideration—more strongly still, must emerge out of—that which white theology has never taken seriously: the black experience.

Whites have claimed the gospel for themselves. They have made the gospel the servant of their own lust for power. God was conceived of as standing unconditionally on the side of whites. God, it was thought, pays no attention to the lies and half-truths of whites ("little white lies"). God, it was thought, pays no attention to the white opposition to and destruction of justice. God, it was thought, graciously approved the white argument for slavery when an argument was necessary (Ham's curse). God's unmistakable blessing rests on apartheid, and on the "Christian" West. The signs of that blessing are visible: wealth and a long and prosperous life—extended by means of a heart transplant in the event that life appears to be too short. It is this Christian West that, regardless of the cost, must be defended against paganism. After all, the white South Africans conquered the Zulus in the Battle of Bloody River. This constitutes the turning point of South African history. This was a battle fought and won for the benefit of the whites and their Christian civilization.[5]

Can the whites succeed? How can they succeed if the gospel itself rejects everything that white society attempts to maintain and defend? How can the whites succeed if the gospel of the liberation that Jesus Christ effects condemns white "Christianity"? Against what paganism does white society struggle if its "Christian civilization" can be maintained only by trampling justice underfoot? This "Christian civilization" is established on self-centeredness, selfishness, murder, and the theft of the land.

In the struggle for the control of India, British Christian officers gave Indians not only Bibles but also bed sheets that had been contaminated by smallpox. This was done to diminish the number of Indians quickly. In this we can recognize clearly the truth of Frantz Fanon's words: "Europe, literally, is the creation of the Third World."

To defend what I have been describing, you must be alienated from the gospel. This has become clear over and over again. If God remains God in spite of all the whites' manipulation, and if the whites recognize that all their economic and military power do not aid them to escape God's consuming judgment, and if the whites are not able to withstand God's redeeming, liberating deeds, then they will be filled with anxiety. History blackmails you: what honest whites can read their history and not be overcome by feelings of guilt? And the path that has been followed no longer appears to be a viable path. What at one time seemed to be brilliant argumentation in favor of that path now seems to be argumentation that leads to its rejection. You cannot carry out your own plan any longer, because your own interests will be threatened. The West is threatened with drowning in its own prosperity. Realization on the part of the white West that money and technology are not all there is has come too late.

In South Africa, even if it were possible, the whites do not dare to implement apartheid consistently. World history moves ahead inexorably. The coup in Portugal shall not be without consequences for the West. Black consciousness cannot be suppressed. The struggle for the liberation and "decolonialization" of our humanity goes on unabatedly. As a result, white anxiety increases. Whites think they can consolidate their own safety by neutralizing and oppressing the symbol of their anxiety: blacks. This oppression, however, creates hate and bitterness that become visible in society. These, in turn, generate increased anxiety and confusion among whites. But this is not a vicious circle. It is, rather, a plunging spiral.

And Haman had the gallows made. . . . Terrible, indeed, Judge.

You Have Seen . . . God's Righteousness and Human Rights

The right to live in God's world as a human being is not the sole right of whites that eventually, through the kindness of whites, can be extended to "deserving" (obsequious?) blacks as a "special privilege." Human dignity for all is a fundamental biblical right. Nevertheless, many whites seem to think that blacks live by the grace of whites. Whites determine who and what we must be. Whites determine what our life shall be like. Whites determine where and how we may live. Whites determine who may be our friends. Whites determine whom we may marry. Whites determine how we shall be educated. Whites determine—insofar as our children receive an education at all—what sort of education our children shall receive. Whites determine the possibilities and the boundaries of our humanity. In this process, *the* criterion always was and still is a skin color: white.

Blacks now wish to make it clear to whites that this whole process is sinful. We can no longer continue to live in this manner without bringing God's consuming wrath upon us. How shall we correct this neglect, this evasion of our responsibility, to realize our humanity, the potential God has structured into us? How it must grieve the Holy Spirit that God's human creation is destroyed, is denigrated to a "thing"—and this in the name of God! How it must, furthermore, grieve the Holy Spirit that *we* have *permitted* this to happen! We, therefore, shall not beg for the right to live as human beings. That we need not do. No one person has the right to take our life in their hands and to exercise the power to give our life to us or to withhold it from us. As Adam Small says:

> We do *not* live by the grace of the whites. . . . Even the "best" whites have thought always that they hold our lives in their hands. Although, therefore, protest shall play a role in our future actions, we must realize, nevertheless, that protest is itself a form of begging. We shall not, I repeat, beg. The primary form of expression shall be the manifestation of our blackness. Over and over again we shall make out blackness visible. We do not exist for the benefit of the whites. We *exist*.[6]

The source of our certainty in this matter is not this or that white promise or, to use modern idiom, necessary concession. The source of our certainty, rather, is God's righteousness, God's justice. The state that wishes to be respectable cannot permit justice to be negated. The state that wishes to be known as "Christian" must be more careful than this. In the Bible there is a close connection among God's love, God's justice or righteousness, and human rights. Black theology maintains that you cannot talk about God's love without talking about God's righteousness or justice. These both assume concrete form in the relationship between God and humankind, and in our interpersonal relationships.

God's love for the people is active, concerned with providing justice for the people and with making the divine justice visible. God's love for Israel is never a romantic or sentimental feeling that may or may not have a focus. God's love for Israel, rather, is startlingly concrete. God hears the grievances of the people and sees the cruelty of its oppressors: "I *know* their sufferings" (Exod. 3:7). God's love means that God chooses in favor of the people and against the oppressor pharaoh; that God makes the lost cause of the people God's own cause. Choosing one side means that it is impossible for God to maintain the status quo. God, in a wonderful manner, becomes involved completely in the liberation of the people.

God acts openly, not secretly. God does this as a challenge to the powers that be and to the powerful ones who think that they can manipulate God's justice, or that they can escape God's judgment. God acts openly so that the world may know that Israel's God lives—lives for the people of Israel; that Yahweh is the liberator of the oppressed and the warrior who fights for justice in behalf of the downtrodden. God is not ashamed to be called "the God of the oppressed." "You have seen what I did to the Egyptians, and that I have borne you up on eagle's wings and have brought you to me" (Exod. 19:4, 5). Of course! You have *seen*!

We can now state the following conclusion: God's righteousness is manifested in liberative deeds. We must add a further point: God's liberation is not an isolated deed, a blinding flash in history that we see today but of which no trace will be found tomorrow. God's liberation, rather, is a movement. It moves through history. Over and over again God is manifested as the warrior who fights for justice. God deals grimly—justly—with the pharaoh who oppresses Israel; but God deals no less grimly—justly—with the wealthy Israelites who offer no justice to their poor fellow Israelites. Israel knew God as earnest and supportive (Isaiah); biting, sarcastic, and angry (Amos); but always unrivaled in struggling for the people, even when unappreciated. God's justice or righteousness, therefore, is the liberation, the healing and salvation, that God wills to realize and actualize among us.

Something more, however, must be said about God's deeds. God performs mighty deeds *and* motivates persons to do the divine will, to do justice. It is no accident that the text I have referred to (Exod. 19:4, 5) is followed by Exodus 20:1—"I am the Lord, your God, who led you out of the house of bondage, out of Egypt." Liberation cannot be dissociated from love. When God uses Hosea to stimulate Israel to remember its liberation, it is God who proclaims a relationship between love and justice: "When Israel was a child, I loved him, and I called my son out of Egypt" (Hos. 11:1).

H. M. Kuitert has demonstrated that in the Bible the terms "justice," "righteousness," and "to do justice" are concepts that are operative in the framework of "the covenantal partnership."[7] You must act in justice vis-à-vis the other if you are to be an authentic covenantal partner of the Other. "To act in justice" contains in it the meaning "to enable others to realize their potential," "to give recognition to the other's humanity." It means "to give recognition to the other's claim to justice." God does not merely liberate; God liberates persons from one situation so that they can live in a new, an appropriate, situation. God liberates persons so that they are able to do justice. This is the basis for the legitimate desire of everyone to live as a whole, real person.

God's justice is the source of black humanity. God's tireless zeal for the liberation of the enslaved and needy is the inspiration for the struggle to liberate blacks. We take the biblical message seriously and we accept it unconditionally—that is, we have faith in, we *believe in*, the God who is the liberator. We believe that God unconditionally establishes justice for the wretched; that God saves the poor; but that God shatters the oppressor (Ps. 72:4). We know that we have been called to freedom (liberation), and that we must persevere in the freedom that Christ has effected for us (Gal. 5:1).

True freedom never consists in fleeing from the world and its problems, in acting as if the only concern of the Christian were "heaven." Countless blacks have been guilty of this in the past—with, I may add, the encouragement of white Christians.

True freedom is not the art of mere survival. This is still a well-known stunt of blacks. South African blacks for a long time, in both speech and action, gave the appearance of being cooperative, addressed meekly all whites as *baas*, "said what the whites wanted to hear," and worked in harmony with the system for the purpose of "getting out of the system what there was to get." Behind the backs of whites, however, blacks for a long time poked fun at them because whites were very stupid. In addition to being dangerous, this is also dishonest. Dishonest persons, moreover, are never free persons.

Black freedom should never be conceived of as a duplication of white, bourgeois individualism. The truly free are those who realize that God is the basis and the guarantee of their freedom. They therefore regard every curtailment of freedom as rebellion against God. They furthermore champion the cause of the oppressed and of freedom. They know, also, that freedom, as is true of justice and love, is not a passive state and status. It, rather, is a movement, an action. God liberates persons, as was said above, so that they can enact and embody justice.

True justice can make covenant partners out of us because justice serves God's *shalom* and creates true community. In the situation in which we live at present, we are not covenant partners. We, rather, are enemies. Justice is not in effect. We are bribed with substitutes for justice. Among us "fellowship" has come to mean, "above all, do not tell the truth." One must pay a price for honesty and real Christian obedience. The price is coercion, ostracism, and exile. Black theology, therefore, is indispensable if we are to penetrate all the sham and to discern the heart of the matter.

The Black Messiah and Black Humanity

True love and true justice, as I have said, enable persons to realize the full potential of their humanity. In this situation a person can be an authentic person. Humanity is extremely important; it is not a general and empty concept that can be given any content one desires. Humanity is an important concept: it functions in the context of God's activity among us. At the center of this activity of God is the Christ-event.

We confess that Jesus Christ embodies true divinity and true humanity. He was human as God intended humans to be. In him God was in the world. In him God was with humankind. In him our being "like God," of necessity, took a clear and distinct form. Subsequently there could be no misunderstanding about what God expects from us.

Our being "like God" has nothing to do with the physical appearance of God. It is meant to indicate how God is God and how we must be what we are. Jesus of Nazareth was the concrete and living image of God. Israel recognized and knew God in God's deeds, in God's "dealings" with and in behalf of the people. In his "dealings" with persons Jesus was the true and authentic reflection of the gracious God in action: "The one who has seen me [in action] has seen the Father [in action]" (John 14:9).[8]

We must raise the following question: What is the meaning of this confession for blacks who are the oppressed of the world? Do we see in Jesus the one to whom we have been introduced through the ages—the romantic preacher who declared a message of submissiveness oriented solely to the future, to heaven? Is Jesus really as "Western" as the "civilization" that claims him? Is the Jesus whom thousands of our ancestors learned to know while they worked on plantations as slaves identified with the power and the oppression of whites? If this picture of Jesus is true and real, then Jesus is white and he is unacceptable to blacks. The Jesus who represented the God of the Bible cannot be the same one whose name was carved into the bows of the Dutch slave ships in which Africans were transported to their death. For black Christians, as James Cone has said, the only authentic confession in our age is the confession of Jesus Christ as the black Messiah.[9]

The image of Jesus that the New Testament presents to us is one that identifies him to a remarkable degree with the black experience. He was poor. At the time of his circumcision, his poor parents were not able to bring the sacrifice prescribed in the law. They brought instead the sacrifice of the poor: two turtledoves in place of a year-old lamb (Lev. 12:6–8; Luke 2:21–24). He maintained the humble status of his birth throughout his life. He belonged to a poor, dispossessed people, without rights in its own land, subjected daily to countless humiliations by foreign oppressors. Jesus lived and worked among the poor. His disciples and followers came from among the poor. He lived a life of solidarity with the poor. He felt at home with the "have-nots" rather than with the "haves." All must admit that his message spoke to the condition of the lowly. His message generated hope and trust among them. And they felt at home with *him*. His message had an effect among the poor. It had little or no positive effect among the rich and the privileged.

Jesus made no secret of the fact that he had come for the lowly—the outcasts, the despised ones, those of whom the rich in their "sophisticated" language would have said, they "are very primitive. If they were to be given freedom in an amiable fashion, they would not live virtuously and would not know how to govern themselves. But even if they live in wretched circumstances, nevertheless, one can expect them to serve one well."[10] This is how the Reformed pastor from Coevorden, the Netherlands, Johan Picardt, wrote about the "kaffirs" in South Africa. But Jesus came for them; not for those who had no need of a physician.

At the very beginning of his public ministry, Jesus made clear what his mission was: "The Spirit of the Lord is upon me, because he has anointed me to bring the good news to the poor. He has sent me to proclaim release to the captives and recovery of sight to the blind, to set at liberty those who are oppressed, to proclaim the acceptable year of the Lord" (Luke 4:18ff.). This program is one in which there is solidarity between Jesus and those he has come to serve. Jesus the oppressed one came and took sides with the oppressed. He came as the forsaken one without form or appearance, a man of sorrows, bowed down with illness (Isa. 53). He knew what it was to live like a hunted animal. He knew what it was to speak with care at all times so as to evade the clutches of "informers." He lived on earth in a way familiar to us blacks. He identified himself completely with us. He is the black Messiah.

In spite of his humble position, however, he still is called Jesus the liberator. He brought a new message to his oppressed people and to everyone who will listen to it: a new message of hope and liberation. He lived among the oppressed with a heavenly radicalism. By so doing he set dynamite to the status quo and to "law and order." The lowly had been "things." They were without value except insofar as they were useful to the Romans and their accomplices. Jesus told them that he loved them; that they were of greater value than the birds and the flowers, even if it was true that Solomon in all his glory lacked their natural splendor. In a country where the Roman fist was the highest authority, Jesus enthroned the human value of the oppressed.

Nor did Jesus practice a "Christian sadism" among his followers. When he was alone with the woman who had been accused of adultery, he did not permit her to bow down on the ground to demonstrate her gratitude. She, rather, was able to assume a responsible role immediately: "Go and from now on sin no more!" (John 8:11).

Jesus protected the lowly from the religious tyranny of the

priests and scribes: the person is more important than the Sabbath; the law functions in the service of the people. Herod, the political tyrant and accomplice of the Romans, Jesus called a "fox." The self-centered Pharisees he called "whitened sepulchers," "hypocrites," "serpents," "a brood of adders." Jesus calls the Pharisees by these names because they "devoured the houses of widows," but "for the sake of appearance" they prayed long prayers, and because they ignored "the weightier" matters of the law: judgment and mercy and fidelity (Matt. 23). He offers liberation to the lowly and establishes their humanity in a radical way. By his royal association with them, he summoned the lowly to claim and to strengthen their own humanity.

We have looked in vain for this Jesus in the preaching of whites. The message we heard there was a completely different message. The message was one of passivity, of glossing over white injustice—a message that assured whites their position always and unconditionally. You need only read the sermons and orations that have been given in South Africa on the "Day of Promise" to understand why one of the publications of the *Pro Veritate* movement speaks about an "Afrikaner gospel" (i.e., a white gospel).[11]

I cannot omit reference to one more example of "gospel proclamation" to emphasize how the ground was prepared for both blacks and whites to view black-white relationships. This example comes from a report of the Dutch pastor M. C. Vos, who migrated to South Africa at the end of the eighteenth century. In his report he tells how he persuaded farmers to permit their slaves to be instructed in the gospel.[12] Keep in mind that he was neither ignorant nor blind to reality:

> "It is natural that your slaves will not become worse but, rather, better through education. Let me try to convince you of this. You have slaves, I have noticed, who originally came from a variety of lands. Put yourself in the place of one of them for a few minutes and think in the following way: I am a poor slave, but I was not born in this status. I was taken from my dear parents, my loving wife or husband, from my children, my brothers and sisters, by human

thieves who kidnaped me and took me away from my own country. I have no hope that I shall ever see one of my family members again. I have been dragged here to this land by tyrants. On the ride to this place, if I had not been in chains and fetters I would have chosen death in preference to life. Here I was sold as an animal. Now I am a slave. I must do everything which is commanded me even to the point of doing very undesirable work. If I do not do this willingly, then I am beaten severely.

"Suppose for a few minutes," the pastor continued in his conversation with the farmer, "that this was the situation in which *you* found yourself. Tell me, if you were to be in that situation, would you have the desire to do your work? Would you not, rather, frequently be despondent, sorrowful, obstinate, and disobedient?"

The man was moved. He said, "I had never thought about that. If I were in the place of one like the one you have described, who knows to what sort of acts of despair I would be driven."

"Well," I continued, "if you permit them to remain stupid and ignorant, upon occasion thoughts of this type will arise and, at times, come to expression in terribly extreme actions. If they are instructed correctly, as they should be, they will be instructed that God rules all things; that nothing happens apart from his rule; that God is a God of order; that in the same way in which they must serve their master and mistress, their master and mistress must serve those who are in positions of authority over them; that those who do not serve obediently are punished either on their body or in their purse. You can make clear to them that that which seems evil to us frequently turns out to our advantage. If they had remained by their friends in their own country, then they would have remained ignorant of the way of salvation until their death; and then, at death, because of this ignorance, they would have been lost forever. Now, however, since they have been brought to a Christian land, they have the opportunity of gaining knowledge of the only Savior who can and shall make them happy through all eternity.

When they begin to understand this a bit, the despondent and grieving thoughts will change. Then they will begin to think: if that is the way things are, then I shall be content with my lot and I shall attempt to do my work obediently and joyfully."

The farmer cried out, "Why weren't we told these things before? I must confess my ignorance. From now on I shall never dissuade anyone from educating his slaves. I, rather, shall persuade everyone to educate their slaves."

Today, of course, different arguments are used. We are all more sophisticated. The heart of the matter, however, is unchanged. The calling and responsibility of black theology is to liberate us from this undesirable "whiteness." Because our blackness, and only our blackness, is the cause of the oppression of the black community, Cone says, "the christological importance of Jesus Christ must be found in his blackness. . . . Taking our cue from the historical Jesus who is pictured in the New Testament as the Oppressed One, what else, except blackness, could adequately tell us the meaning of his presence today?"[13] Today, just as yesterday, he has taken the sorrow of his people upon himself. He has become for them everything that is necessary for their liberation. For us Jesus is the black Messiah and the irrevocable guarantee of our black humanity.

Black Theology, Black Identity, and the Future

Black theology, as I have said, seeks a breakthrough so that it can expose the true human person, the authentic being of humanity. And, once more, *our* true humanity consists precisely in our creation as black. We shall never be able to gain better human relations until whites have learned to accept blacks *as black persons*, and to give themselves in service to them.

Let me state the matter very clearly: when we speak about the affirmation of our blackness, the affirmation of our creation as black, it has nothing to do with *being resigned to* our blackness. It is precisely what I indicated that it is: the affirmation of our blackness, the affirmation of our creation as black. *Black is beautiful.*

We speak about a rebirth, a re-creation, a renewal, a reevaluation of our self. In this connection black theology frequently uses the word *self-love*. Some interpret this to mean: "love for the black and hate for the white." I offer no apology here, because we need not discuss every white absurdity, but I do wish to say one thing: Jesus did not prescribe a law when he gave his followers the commandment to love your neighbor "*as yourself.*" He began with a fact that is universally accepted. Everyone values one's own self. Everyone desires to live a life that has significance and value. Everyone is driven to preserve one's own self.

There are, however, circumstances that work such destruction of one's self that even this fundamental human drive is lacking. Persons under severe pressure can build up a devastating contempt for their own self. This was the lot of blacks. Slavery, domination by others, total dependence, lack of legal rights and the status of an alien whether in one's own land or in another land, discrimination and humiliation—all have had a devastating influence on the spiritual life of blacks. In the society dominated by whites, "white" was the acme of all that was "good"; "black" was the symbol of everything that was of little value or status.

In America, blacks scarcely survived the assault on their traditions and history. In South Africa blacks were said to have had no history. South Africa "arose" first in 1652, and the only traditions that may continue to operate are the "nondangerous" ones.

What whites, consciously or unconsciously, think about blacks need not be repeated here. Martin Luther King, Jr., said that in *Roget's Thesaurus of English Words and Phrases*, a standard American reference work, there are no less than 120 synonyms for "black," and at least 60 of them are offensive. "Black" is "dirty," "demonic," "angry," etc. The same dictionary, on the other hand, contains 134 synonyms for "white," and every one of them is favorable. The standard Afrikaans-English dictionary (*Het Groot Afrikaans/Engels*) still teaches students that the correct translation of "black person"is *swartnerf* ("black vein") or *swartslang* ("black snake"). The latter word is a collective noun that translates the term "natives." Black children, furthermore, must use the same dictionary and must learn that the English word "gentleman" is translated into Afrikaans by the word "white man" (*witman*). When you, furthermore, discover that "gentle" is defined in terms of "respectable," "civilized," "loving," and "skillful," then both the meaning of the word and its implications are very clear. *Van Dale*, the standard Dutch dictionary, represents no improvement. It is no wonder then, is it, that the blacks have learned to hate and despise themselves? And I have said almost nothing about the systematic veneration of whites and the scorn for blacks that are perpetuated by the countless apartheid laws.

South African blacks are now searching for their true humanity: a "decolonialized" humanity free from the infection of white scorn and contempt. This does not mean, of course, that blacks inevitably will hate whites. It means that blacks simply shall not accept any longer a "brotherhood" in which the one brother, the black, must be a slave and the other brother, the white, must be the master. We find it intolerable that this hypocrisy, this inauthenticity, continues under the banner "Christian." Any form of white oppression is equally intolerable. White values shall no longer be thought of as "the highest good." Blacks shall no longer hate themselves and wish that they were white. No longer shall blacks define themselves in terms of others. They shall, rather, move toward their own authentic blackness out of their Negroid and nonwhite character. In this way they shall force whites to see themselves in their whiteness and to perceive the consequences of this whiteness for others.

This is the meaning of black self-love. We will hate no whites simply because they are white. We hate their oppression, their enslavement of others. As long as they desire to be oppressors they cannot be coequals. The choice is theirs. We will live without any apology or defense, and we will not make any excuse for our existence, or beg for what is our birthright. We are not eager to hate whites; we wish to treat them as human beings. If this causes whites to panic, that is their problem.

Black theology wishes to proclaim this message of authenticity to whites. Future generations of both blacks and whites may not have to learn and embody a theology that is nothing other than an extension of cultural imperialism (Rubem Alves). Our theology must concern itself with authentic questions, with the true liberation of the unliberated. In our theology, we must dare to limit ourselves to that which is most urgent and most authentic. The criteria of urgency and authenticity make it all the more foolish, even in the West, for Christians to run around making a great fuss and much ado about their love for their neighbors. In this connection, Cardonnel writes about the parable of the good Samaritan:

> The essential difference between, on the one hand, the Samaritan, the common man, the man of the people, the man who disappears in the crowd, and, on the other hand, the priests, the economists, the psychologists, and the experts in power and authority lies in this: the first-named needed no religion, no doctrine or precise definition of his field of labor, in order to love, in order to exercise empathy, in order to act in a loving fashion and to experience solidarity with the other.[14]

The man from Samaria, however, first appeared in the parable after the injured man's struggle was ended, when everything was over. At this point Cardonnel raises the real question that theology must raise: What will happen if love is expressed during the struggle, not after the struggle?[15]

In this situation black theology wishes to be present in the role of a servant. Black theology wishes to cooperate in addressing urgent and authentic questions without any anxiety. Only in this way shall we achieve authentic community. Black theology wishes to make operative what was holy in the black African community long before whites came on the scene: unity, mutual respect, community. It is alarming that this element of community has been virtually absent as long as we have known one another—that is, as long as blacks have known the Christian faith. This community is not openly available to be seized whenever one happens to desire it. Community, rather, lies on the far side of much struggle and doubt, of mutual trust and courage. For us this is the courage to be black.

This community located on the far side of struggle is not to be regarded as an eschatological event, at present only an incomprehensible chimera; it is, rather, as real as Africa itself. There is a centuries-old proverb in the language of the Tumbuka: *Muntu ni munta cifukwa cabanyake*—"A person is a person only because of others and in behalf of others." This is the objective toward which we wish to move.

Chapter II

The Black Church and the Future

I was rather surprised when your secretary general asked me to address you on this subject. It suggests that the need to speak of a black church is not confined to those in the traditional black churches alone; blacks in the so-called multiracial churches may no longer be excluded.

This is a happy development, because it means that in spite of so many problems and reverses, the real meaning and significance of black consciousness has not completely bypassed the Christian church.

Black theology teaches us that theology cannot be done in a void. It is always done within a particular situation. The situation of blackness in South Africa is the unavoidable context within which the theological reflection of black Christians takes place. We have come to realize that persons are influenced by their social and economic environment, and that their thinking is influenced by the social conditions in which they live. We recognize that Christians living in different situations will have different understandings of life, as well as vastly different understandings of the gospel and its demands on their lives. This is basically why for some the gospel is an incomparable message of liberation, where-

This is the address that Allan Boesak gave to the national conference of the South African Council of Churches in July 1979. The text has been edited for inclusion in the present collection.

as others find in it justification for a system that exploits and oppresses.

Black theology is a black understanding of the gospel. This understanding is not confined to one group or denomination only, nor is it an automatic universal revelation to all blacks. It is rather the result of a painful, soul-searching struggle of black Christians with God and with the meaning of God's word for their lives today. These black Christians have wrestled with black history—a history of suffering, degradation, and humiliation caused by white racism. They have taken seriously the cry of many blacks who, through the years, refused to believe that the gospel could corroborate the narrow, racist ideology that white Christians were yelling from black pulpits and that white theologians were giving respectability to in their learned books.

These black Christians were the ones who refused to accept an anemic gospel of subservience and dejection—both in the blatant forms of a hundred years ago and in the subtler forms of the present. Somehow they always knew that the God of the exodus and the covenant, the God of Jesus Christ, was different from the God whom whites were proclaiming. It was when they understood this that they walked out of the established, white-controlled churches to form their own church. It was then that they rejected white theology and went in search of a God "who walks with feet among you, who has hands to heal, a God who sees you—a God who loves and has compassion," to quote that great leader of one of the first African independent churches, Isaiah Shembe.

Those black Christians knew that the gospel of Jesus Christ does not deny the struggle for black humanity, and it was with this light from God's word that they went into the struggle, both within the church and outside it. And it is this understanding that today inspires many black Christians in their search for authentic humanity and a true Christian church.

Out of this struggle, more than two centuries old, emerged the black church, a broad movement of black Christians, joined in a black solidarity that transcends all barriers of denomination and ethnicity. It shares the same black experience, the same understanding of suffering and oppression, and the same common goal of liberation from all forms of oppression. It is a movement deeply imbued with the belief that the gospel of Jesus Christ proclaims the total liberation of all peoples, and that the God and Father of Jesus Christ is the God of the oppressed.

There is another point I wish to make. We must remember that in situations such as ours blackness (a state of oppression) is not only a color; it is a *condition*. And it is within this perspective that the role of white Christians should be seen. Certainly I do not refer to those whites who for so long have been leaders in the black churches. Nor do I refer to those who happen to be in control of churches where blacks are the majority. I speak of those white Christians who have understood their own guilt in the oppression of blacks in terms of corporate responsibility, who have genuinely repented and have been genuinely converted; those whites who have clearly committed themselves to the struggle for liberation and who, through their commitment, have taken upon themselves the *condition* of blackness in South Africa. In a real sense, they "bear the marks of Christ." They are part of the black church, not as lords and masters but as servants, not as "liberals" but as brothers and sisters, for they have learned not so much to do *for* blacks, but to identify with what blacks are doing to secure their liberation.

This is the black church, and it is about this church that I shall be concerned here. Before I can begin to talk about the black church and the future, however, I shall have to look at our present situation.

The Struggle of the Black Church

What is the position of the black church in South Africa today? It is a church that has been uncertain of its identity. The black church in South Africa has not yet succeeded in attaining for itself an authentic identity. In many cases, white control is still a reality and that makes it difficult for blacks to identify with the church. By "white control" I do not mean only administrative control—although it is important who decides and really speaks for the church—I am also thinking of the predominantly white image of the black church: in style, in witness, in commitment.

The structures that blacks have inherited are geared to the

needs of those who have no sensitivity whatsoever to the black situation. It is no wonder, then, that the black church sometimes finds it hard to respond meaningfully to blacks in need of God's presence in their lives. A precondition for the authentic identity of the black church is the ability to identify with the community it serves. The black church must identify with the past, present, and future of the community that it serves. The black church must become part of that community, so that it may understand the joys, sorrows, and aspirations of that community. And the church must not be afraid to identify with the struggle of the people. For the struggle in South Africa is not merely political; it is also moral. The struggle is not merely *against* an oppressive political and exploitative economic system; it is also a struggle *for* the authenticity of the gospel of Jesus Christ. The struggle is as much against a political philosophy and practice as it is against a pseudo-religious ideology.

Apartheid and all it stands for is not a system that places its fortunes on the political judgment of a people. It demands, with idolatrous authority, a subservience and obedience in all spheres of life that a Christian can give only to God. (Of course, this in itself is not strange; apartheid shares this demand with all other totalitarian forms of government.)

To identify with the struggle is to realize that the struggle for liberation and the attainment of black humanity are commensurate with the gospel of Jesus Christ. It does not mean that the Christian has to condone and justify everything in the course of the struggle. It does mean, however, that in the struggle the Christian has the duty to be the salt of the earth and the light of the world. One may legitimately ask, of course, if Christians can stand aside and allow the struggle for our liberation to be monopolized by those who do not believe in the Lord Jesus Christ, for we know that God will hear the cry of the oppressed, "How long, O Lord?"

None other than John Calvin reminded us of this when he wrote:

> Tyrants and their cruelty cannot be endured without great weariness and sorrow. . . . Hence almost the whole world sounds forth these words, How long, How long? When any-

> one disturbs the whole world by his ambition and avarice, or everywhere commits plunders, or oppresses miserable nations, when he distresses the innocent, all cry out, How long? And this cry, proceeding as it does from the feeling of nature and the dictate of justice, is at length heard by the Lord. . . . [The oppressed] know that this confusion of order and justice is not to be endured. *And this feeling, is it not implanted in us by the Lord? It is then the same as though God heard himself, when he hears the cries and groanings of those who cannot bear injustice.*[1]

Of course, Calvin is right. So, although acknowledging that the powers of the anti-Christ are at work in every situation, the black church knows full well that refusal to participate in this struggle constitutes an act of disobedience to God. We know also that where true human liberation takes place, it takes place because Christ is there.

In the heat of the struggle Christians today are called to be the light of the world. In the midst of the struggle we are called to be the embodiment of God's ideal for this broken world. Christians must be there to represent God's possibilities for authentic Christian love, meaningful reconciliation, and genuine peace.

In arguing thus, I cannot urge that the black church be absorbed by the world, or that the struggle dictate to the church. It remains true that only a critical differentiation between the church and the world—that is, adhering to the criteria of the gospel of its Lord—will enable the church to make a meaningful contribution in keeping God's options open to those who in the thick of battle, because of their tears, their fear, or their anger, often fail to recognize these options. It is not a Christian struggle I am pleading for, but a Christian presence in the struggle.

A Crucial Decision

This decision is not one that will face us some time in the future. It is facing us now. The church is facing a tremendous challenge. In the last decade or two, there have been profound and rapid changes in the black community in South Africa. These are not so much changes in tangible political structures as changes in political consciousness, which reached a peak in 1976.

Not all the young persons who were prominent at that time have left the church. Some of them have done so—in disappointment and disgust. Many, however, with their parents, are still in the church, but with a highly sensitized political consciousness and with probing, critical questions about the nature and the witness of the church. These are young persons with experience far beyond their years, experience born of their active and personal engagement in the struggle for liberation and for their God-given humanity. It is my contention that the black church does not yet know how to deal with this new generation.

This new political consciousness, and the consciousness of black humanity, have brought a new sense of responsibility in the black community. This new sense of responsibility and the active involvement of the black community in the struggle have taken away almost completely the traditional deference to the church. Church officials are no longer judged by their office and the authority it represents; their office and authority are now measured by their active participation in the struggle for liberation. I daresay that although this worries us no end, we have yet to come to terms with this change of attitude.

Between Two Theologies

The black church is dependent on an alien theology. This I regard as very serious. At the basis of so many maladies in the black church—our inadequate lifestyle, dependence on white resources, the very acceptance and rationalization of the situation that makes us so dependent—lies our dependence on an alien theology.

For centuries the black church has been engaged in a struggle to speak truthfully. In this struggle, two theologies were fighting for supremacy within its ranks. On the one hand, there has been the theology we have inherited from Western Christianity: the theology of accommodation and acquiescence. It engendered an individualistic, other-worldly spirituality that had no interest in the realities of this world except to proclaim the existing order as the God-ordained order. This theology wanted blacks to accept slavery and, in modern times, their lowly position as second- and third-class citizens. Either through force of circumstance or through sheer hopelessness, blacks accepted this anemic, heaven-oriented theology, still rampant in the black church today.

On the other hand, there was also a theology of refusal: a theology that refused to accept that God was just another word for the status quo; a theology that understood that the God of the Bible is a God who takes sides with the oppressed and who calls persons to participate in the struggle for liberation and justice in the world. This was a theology that understood God's love for the lowly and therefore uttered a clear "no!" against those who oppressed and dehumanized them—whether on slave farms or native reserves, whether in the aseptic and air-conditioned temples of banks and boardrooms or within those dark and awesome prison buildings where so many brothers and sisters have lost their souls . . . and their lives.

This theology of refusal has been the theology of great black leaders: to name but a few, Denmark Vesey, Frederick Douglass, W. E. B. Dubois, Martin Luther King, Jr., Nehemiah Tile, Mangana Mokone, and Albert Luthuli. This theology was expressed masterfully by Frederick Douglass:

> I love the religion of our blessed Savior. I love that religion which comes from above, in the wisdom of God which is first pure, then peaceable, gentle . . . without partiality and without hypocrisy. . . . I love that religion which is based upon that glorious principle of love to God and love to man, which makes its followers do unto others as they themselves would be done by others. . . . It is because I love this religion that I hate the slave-holding, woman-whipping, the mind-darkening, the soul-destroying religion that exists in America. . . . Loving the one I must hate the other; holding to one I must reject the other.

This is the theology the black church must make its own if it is to survive, if it is to become truly "church." We must come to understand that this faith is not a "new," "politicized" faith, but rather the age-old gospel. It is the message of the Torah and the prophets. It is a message that unmasks the sinfulness of humanity, in personal life as well as in the existing social, political, and economic structures. It is a message that judges, but it also speaks of hope, of conversion, of redemption. It is a message for the whole of life. And it is our task to bring this message to our people in such a way that it makes sense in the de facto situation.

Confrontation with the State

In the light of what has been stated above, a profound question emerges. What about the future?

Basically there are two alternatives facing our country. One is to continue with the present trend of modernizing and modifying white *baasskap* ("dominance," "supremacy") and eventually to end up with a civil war; the other is to bring about radical and fundamental change that would inspire the search for a truly new society.

At the same time, the black church has two choices. It can develop a policy of realpolitik and accommodation, urging the people to accept piecemeal concessions, and making it thereby easy for itself; or it can stand firm, challenging the forces of the status quo and accepting the risks that come with it.

We should not deceive ourselves. This choice will not be easy. Now that all meaningful black organizations have been banned, the black church has become more important than ever before as a vehicle for expressing the legitimate aspirations of blacks. The government knows this. That is why the government is going to concentrate its repressive measures on the church more and more.

If the black church is going to be true to its Christ and its calling, I can see no way that confrontation between the black church and the white state can be avoided. The government may also, however, try to persuade the black church that real changes are indeed taking place, and that, for the sake of peace, the black church should accept them. I think that we must expect a time when government officials will more and more employ a kind of Christian language, using such terms as "love," "peace," and "reconciliation," for the purpose of undermining the watchfulness of the church. And many blacks, the so-called privileged underprivileged, may discover that the government is extending more privileges to them, and they may try to pressure the black church.

The black church is called to be wide awake, to remember to take as its criterion not the privileges of those who already have more than others, but the justice or injustice done to "the least of the brethren." The black church must remember always that an evil system cannot be modified. It must be eradicated.

The second choice of course is the more difficult one. It will leave no room for compromise. It is bound to bring confrontation, not only with the government, but also with those Christians, white and black alike, who shout "peace! peace!" where there is no peace. It will make the black church even more vulnerable. The government will accuse the church of subversion, and some Christians may shout charges of lovelessness and intransigence. In the end, however, the church will have preserved its integrity. The black church, like Moses, is not called to negotiate with the pharaoh. It is called simply to convey the *Lord's* command: Let my people go!

Shunning "Cheap Grace"

I want to suggest a few things the black church must do in order to equip itself for the future.

First of all, we must reaffirm our commitment to Jesus Christ. For the black church, Jesus Christ is Lord. He is Lord over all of life. This confession we must cling to at all costs. Our loyalty and obedience are to him alone. If the black church is to have any future at all, this is where we must be firm. Our allegiance is ultimately not to the laws of the state, or to the laws of self-preservation, but to the commands of the living God. Our loyalty is to Christ. Our criteria are the demands of his kingdom. We shall have to learn not to be dictated to by the demands of the status quo, however intimidating; or by the demands of any ideology, however tempting. Our faith in Jesus Christ and the liberating power of his gospel must form the basis upon which we offer ourselves as a humble servant in the world.

Secondly, we shall have to learn to resist the temptation of what that great theologian of the resistance, Dietrich Bonhoeffer, has called "cheap grace." Love, peace, reconciliation, justice are evangelical realities the black church dare not ignore. But there is a danger in our South African Christianity today. Christians are sometimes so desperate for something "good" to happen in this quagmire of political hopelessness that often they cannnot distinguish between subterfuge and authenticity. In such a situation, it is very tempting to see peace and reconciliation where there is none at all.

Reconciliation and Confrontation

Oppression of blacks in this country has been going on for three hundred years. In the course of those years, humiliation and degradation have left their mark on the souls of millions. Self-hatred and dejection have become the hereditary burden of countless generations. Many have died; many more will die. Distrust, suspicion, hatred have become part of our lives. Therefore, reconciliation is essential. But it will be costly.

In the process of reconciling God with the world, confrontation with evil almost made Christ give up. But it was necessary. It was necessary to unmask human nature for what it really was. It was necessary to rip to shreds the flimsy garment of pseudo-innocence that human beings had wrapped around themselves to convince themselves that they were guiltless.

True reconciliation cannot take place without confrontation. Reconciliation is not feeling good; it is coming to grips with evil. In order to reconcile, Christ had to die. We must not deceive ourselves. Reconciliation does not mean holding hands and singing: "black and white together." It means, rather, death and suffering, giving up one's life for the sake of the other. If white and black Christians fail to understand this, we shall not be truly reconciled.

So it is with peace. One is not at peace with God and one's neighbor because one has succeeded in closing one's eyes to the realities of evil. Neither is peace a situation where terrorism of the defenseless is acceptable because it is being done under the guise of the law. For in South Africa, Adam Small's question remains pertinent: "Which law? Man's law, God's law, devil's law?" Peace is not simply the absence of war or an uneasy quiet in the townships. Peace is the active presence of justice. It is shalom, the well-being of all.

If our theology fails to make clear that Christian love is not a sentimental feeling but an act of justice, doing what is right, our theology does not reflect the gospel fully. We must not be afraid to say that in the South African situation Christian love between white and black must be translated into terms of political, social, and economic justice. By doing this, we help the Christian church to accept the challenge of veracity. Even though this process will be a very painful one, it will prove to be rewarding in the attempt to generate an authentic Christian community.

Thirdly, we must be prepared to meet the challenges the new situation will present. There will be the challenge to preach a relevant gospel to the black community. For many of our young blacks throughout this land, the crucial question is whether the gospel is indeed the gospel of liberation, and not merely a tool for the oppression of the poor. This is a challenge only the black church can meet.

There is also the challenge to find a way of participating meaningfully in the struggle. Words and statements will no longer suffice. With tragic inevitability, the violence inherent in the system of oppression in South Africa breeds violence and counterviolence. In addition, as peaceful protest is made increasingly impossible, the belief grows that violence is the only solution. I realize that the issue of violence is a touchy one, and this is not the place to discuss it. I want to say, however, that the unbelievable hypocrisy of white Christians on this matter is appalling, and it will take all our resources to undo the damage done to Christian integrity on this point.

Although the debate is not yet closed, and although we may be faced with even more taxing situations, we must in the meantime refuse to be idle. The church must initiate and support meaningful pressure on the entrenched system, as a nonviolent way of bringing about change. The church must initiate and support programs of civil disobedience on a massive scale and challenge white

Christians especially on this issue. It no longer suffices to make statements condemning unjust laws and then tomorrow to obey those laws as if nothing were amiss. The time has come for the black church to tell the government and its supporters: we can not in all good conscience obey your unjust laws, because non-cooperation with evil is as much a moral obligation as is cooperation with good. So we will teach our people what it means to obey God rather than man in South Africa. A new study on the investment problem will not suffice. But direct and forceful action will show multinational corporations how serious the church really is about the plight of our people.

To do all this in South Africa is to expect trouble. The repressive, intolerant nature of the present government cannot allow it. And yet the church has no other option. And when we do this we must prepare ourselves for even greater suffering. It is the Lord himself who warned us: "A servant is not greater than his master." For the black church this word of our Lord is especially true: "He who wants to hold onto his life at all costs shall lose it. But he who loses his life for my sake, shall gain it." If the black church can understand this, we shall not have to fear the future.

I pray that the black church in South Africa will, by the grace of God, be truly the church of Christ:

- in the midst of struggle and in the heat of the battle—be a servant church;
- in the midst of violence, oppression, and hatred—be a prophetic church;
- in the midst of hopelessness and pain—be a hopeful church;
- in the midst of compromise—be a committed church;
- in the midst of bondage and fear—be a liberated church;
- in the midst of intimidation and silence—be a witnessing church;
- in the midst of suffering and death—be a liberating church;
- in the midst of failure and disappointment—be a believing church.

To God, the only God, who saves us through Jesus Christ our Lord, be the glory, majesty, authority, and power from all eternity, now and forever!

Chapter III

Divine Obedience: A Letter to the Minister of Justice

The South African Council of Churches (SACC) convened in St. Peter's Church in Hammanskrall, South Africa, in July 1979. The theme of this meeting was "The Church and the Alternative Society." For Allan Boesak's keynote address at the meeting, see chapter 2 in this book. The SACC adopted a resolution in which Christians were encouraged to engage in acts of civil disobedience relative to the apartheid laws. This resolution was not related directly to Dr. Boesak's presentation, although his address does, of course, provide a theological rationale for civil disobedience. Minister Schlebusch responded to this resolution with a warning in which he stated that the South African government was becoming impatient with such statements as the SACC resolution because they "posed a threat to the stability of South African society." In response to the warning of Minister Schlebusch, Dr. Boesak wrote the letter that is the text of this chapter.

This open letter appeared first, in Afrikaans, in *Deurbraak*, Oct./Nov. 1979, pp. 6–8. An abridged English translation appeared in *One World* 50 (Oct. 1979) 9–10; a similar, abridged English translation appeared in *Christianity and Crisis* 39 (Nov. 26, 1979) 298–300. This chapter presents the author's own translation of the unabridged letter to the minister of justice of the Republic of South Africa, Alwyn Schlebusch.

August 24, 1979

The Honourable A. Schlebusch
Minister of Justice
Union Buildings
Pretoria

Dear Sir,

A short while ago you thought it your duty to address the South African Council of Churches, as well as church leaders, very sharply and seriously over radio and television and in the press in connection with the SACC resolution on civil disobedience. Although the resolution was not taken as a direct result of my address, I did express my point of view openly on that occasion and I am one of those who support the SACC in this respect.

You are the minister of justice and it is in this capacity that you have issued your serious warning. I take your words seriously. Hence my reaction, which I express to you respectfully and which I ask you to read as a personal declaration of faith.

Your warning has become almost routine in South Africa: the government continually says to pastors and churches that they must keep themselves "out of politics" and confine themselves to their "proper task": the preaching of the gospel.

However, on this very point an extremely important question emerges: What is the gospel of Jesus Christ that the churches have been called to preach? Surely it is the message of the salvation of God that has come to all peoples in Jesus Christ. It is the proclamation of the kingdom of God and of the lordship of Jesus Christ. But this salvation is the liberation, the making whole, of the *whole person*. It is not something meant for the "inner life," the soul, only. It is meant for the whole of human existence. This Jesus who is proclaimed by the church was certainly not a spiritual being with spiritual qualities estranged from the realities of our human existence. No, he was the Word become flesh, who took on complete human form, and his message of liberation is meant for persons in their *full humanity*.

Besides, the fact that the term "kingdom" is such a political term must already say a great deal to us. For example, this fact brought Reformed Christians to believe (and rightly so) and profess with conviction throughout the centuries that this lordship of Jesus Christ applies to all spheres of life. There is not one inch of life that is not claimed by the lordship of Jesus Christ. This includes the political, social, and economic spheres. The Lord rules over all these spheres, and the church and the Christian proclaim his sovereignty in all these spheres. Surely it is the holy duty and the calling of every Christian to participate in politics so that there also God's law and justice may prevail, and there also obedience to God and God's word can be shown.

The Dutch Reformed Church professes this in its report "Race Relations in the South African Situation in the Light of Scripture." The report states plainly that in its proclamation the church must appeal to its members to apply the principles of the kingdom of God in the social and political sphere. When the word of God demands it, the church is compelled to fulfill its prophetic function vis-à-vis the state *even in spite of popular opinion*. The witness of the church with regard to the government is a part of its essential being in the world, says the report. This is sound Reformed thinking, and the Dutch Reformed Church accepts this because it wants to be Reformed. Why, then, are you refusing to grant other churches and Christians (also other Reformed Christians!) this witness and participation?

But there is still another problem. Through its spokesmen your government has often warned that those of us who serve in the church must "keep out of politics." Yet at the same time it is your own colleagues in the cabinet who want to involve the clergy in political dialogue!

The only conclusion that I can come to is that you do not really object in principle to the participation of the clergy in politics—as long as it happens on *your* terms and within the framework of *your* policy. This seems to me to be neither tenable nor honest. In addition, are you not denying your own history by holding to this viewpoint? Did not the Afrikaner clergy speak as leaders of their people, and did they not inspire their people in what you saw as a just struggle? Did not the churches of the Afrikaner, even in the Anglo-Boer War, stand right in the midst of the struggle? Why, then, do you reject today with a sort of political pietism that which yesterday and the day before you accepted and embraced with thankfulness to God?

But, Mr. Minister, there is even more in your warning, which I cannot ignore. It has to do with the exceptionally difficult and sensitive issue of the Christian's obedience to the government.

It is important that you understand clearly that I have made my call for civil disobedience as a Christian, and that I was addressing the church. The context and basis of my call may thus not be alienated from my convictions as a Christian addressing other Christians upon that same basis.

It surprises me that some have tried to interpret this as a call for wanton violence. It is precisely an *alternative* to violence! And I turn to this alternative because I still find it difficult to accept violence as an unobjectionable solution. Or perhaps there are some who fear that should Christians in South Africa perform their duty in being more obedient to God than to humans, the idolized nature of this state will be exposed. Surely a state that accepts the supreme rule of Christ should not have to be afraid of this?

I believe I have done nothing more than to place myself squarely within the Reformed tradition as that tradition has always understood sacred scripture on these matters.

Essential to this is the following: It is my conviction that, for a Christian, obedience to the state or any earthly authority is always linked to our obedience to God. That is to say, obedience to human institutions (and to human beings) is always relative. The human institution can never have the same authority as God, and human laws must always be subordinate to the word of God. This is how the Christian understands it. Even God does not expect blind servility; Christians cannot even think of giving unconditional obedience to a government.

Our past experience has taught us that this is exactly the kind of obedience, blind and unquestioning, that your government expects. I want, however, to be honest with you: this I cannot give you. The believer in Christ not only has the right, but also the responsibility, should a government deviate from God's law, to be more obedient to God than to the government. The question is not really whether Christians have the courage to disobey the government, but whether we have the courage to set aside God's word and not obey *God*.

Over the years, nearly all the Christian churches in this country have condemned the policies of your government as wrong and sinful. My own church, the Dutch Reformed Mission Church, last year at its synod condemned apartheid as being "in conflict with the gospel of Jesus Christ," a policy that cannot stand up to the demands of the gospel. I heartily endorse this stand my church has taken. Your policy is unjust; it denies persons their basic human rights, and it undermines their God-given human dignity. Too many of the laws you make are blatantly in conflict with the word of God.

I have no doubt that your policies, and their execution, are a tremendous obstacle to reconciliation between the peoples of South Africa. There are laws that are most hurtful, or more draconian than others, and these especially have been condemned by the churches. Now the churches have reached a point where we have to say: If we condemn laws on the grounds of the word of God, how can we obey those laws?

In my view, Christians in South Africa today do not stand alone in this decision. Scripture knows of disobedience to earthly powers when these powers disregarded the Word of the living God. Daniel disobeyed the king's law when he refused to bow down before the graven image of Nebuchadnezzar (Dan. 3: 17–18), because he regarded the king's law as being in conflict with the demands of his God. Peter's refusal to obey the commands of the Sanhedrin not to give witness to Jesus has always been the classic example of disobedience to a worldly authority. To this day his answer still resounds like a bell in the church of Christ: "We must obey God rather than men" (Acts 5:29). There are other examples. Paul displayed nothing of a servile obedience when the magistrates of Philippi wanted to release him from prison after having confined him unlawfully (without a trial!): "They gave us a public flogging, though we are Roman citizens and have not been found guilty; they threw us into prison, and are they now to smuggle us out privately? No, indeed!" (Acts 16:37).

In the case of Peter and John, the Sanhedrin was the highest authority, not only in religious matters, but in everything that did not lie directly in the sphere of the Roman procurator. In the case of Paul, the magistrates were the highest officials in the Roman colony of Philippi. For both Peter and Paul it was clear that occasions could arise where disobedience to unjust authority was the only honorable way for the Christian.

Furthermore, Luke 23:6–12, Mark 15:1–5, and John 18:8–11 teach us that Jesus himself did not always demonstrate obedience to state authority. Before Herod, on one occasion, "he answered him not a word." Also before Pilate there were those moments when he chose to give reply neither to the questions of Pilate, nor to the charges of the high priests and scribes. John tells us something else of great significance. He tells us that Jesus reminded Pilate of something that every bearer of authority must remember or be reminded of: " 'You would have no authority over me at all,' Jesus replied, 'if it had not been granted you from above' " (John 29:11).

I am not arguing that there is "proof" from these actions of Jesus, Peter, and Paul that violent, revolutionary overthrow of a government is justifiable. That is a completely different issue. I am saying, rather, that blind obedience to civil authorities is alien to the Bible; and that, for the Christian, loyalty and obedience to God are first and foremost. May I also point out, parenthetically, that the issue on which everything hinges, and the lesson that South Africa has to learn, is that what is needed is *not* servile submissiveness of citizens to the state, but *rightful co-responsibility* for the affairs of the state? And this is precisely what your policy denies millions of South Africans.

This is not the place to present a full treatment of Romans 13. However, I would simply point out that the first verse of Romans 13, which is often taken as unconditional legitimization of a government's contention that its authority can never be challenged by Christians, is in fact a very serious criticism of that very authority. A government wields authority because, and as long as, it reflects the authority of God. And the power of God is a liberating, creative, serving power. Thus Paul can refer to civil authority as "a servant of God [*diakonos!*] for your good." Thus, throughout the years, it has been taken for granted in Reformed thinking that a government has authority as long as there is evidence that it accepts responsibility for justice, for what is right.

Put another way, the definition of government in Romans 13 does not simply point out that civil authority exists. It also suggests that there is proper authority only where there is a clear distinction between good and evil, so that it is not only important whether a government is "Christian" or not, but really whether it is still truly *government*—that is, understands the difference between good and evil. Where there is no justice and no understanding, the authority of the government is no longer derived from God, but is in conflict with God. Resistance to such a government is both demanded and justified.

Even Augustine, one of the respected fathers of the church, who was concerned particularly with protecting the state and who defended political authority with extraordinary energy, had this to say: "Justice is the only thing that can give worth to a worldly power. What is worldly government if justice is lacking? It is nothing other than a bunch of plunderers."

Calvin echoed this sentiment when he wrote to King Francis in the letter published as the prologue to his *Institutes*: "For where the glory of God is not made the end of the government, it is not a legitimate sovereignty, but a usurpation." And Calvin added, "Where there is no vision, the people perish." Calvin also stated clearly that "worldly princes" lose all their power when they rise up against God. Christians should resist such a power, not obey it.

When, precisely, do the actions of a government collide with the demands of the word of God? In deciding this, the church should be led by the word itself, knowing the demands for justice and peace, and also by the actual experience of the people. It is in the concrete situations of actual human experience that the word of God shows itself alive and more powerful and sharper than any two-edged sword.

In making this decision, the church should look for criteria not among those who make the laws and who have political and economic power, nor among those who are favored by unjust laws, but rather among those who are disadvantaged by these laws, who are hurt at the deepest level of their being: those who suffer, those who have no voice—the oppressed, the "least of these my brethren." And in the eyes of the least of the brethren in our country, your government and your policies stand condemned. I need not repeat these accusations; I simply want to draw your attention to them, and to the truth that is in them.

The untold suffering of men, women, and children, the bitterness of too many, the wounds caused by your policy through the years can never be forgotten, nor compensated for by the "concessions" your government is apparently willing to make. The superficial adjustments to apartheid already initiated do not touch the root of the matter. It is as one of your colleagues has said: "The fact that a black man is allowed to wear a *Springbok* emblem (as he participates in multiracial sports) does not give him political rights." Indeed, and we may add: it does not give him his God-given humanity either.

You complain that the churches are "against the government." But it is because of your policies that so many churches and so many Christians find themselves against you. In this, we really have no choice, because the church of Christ in South Africa *must* obey God rather than you. I plead with you: stop your disastrous policies.

May I end with a personal word? I am not writing this letter in order to be brave or arrogant. I must honestly confess that I am afraid of you. You are the minister of justice. As such, you have at your disposal awesome powers such as only a fool would underestimate. The victims of these powers are sown across the path of the past and recent history of South Africa.

I, like any other South African, want to live a normal life with my wife and children. I want to serve the church without fear. I want a country where freedom is seen as the right of every citizen and not as a gift to be given or withheld by the government. I want, along with millions of our people, to have co-responsibility for government in our native land, with everything you want for yourself and your children. I, too, want peace, but authentic peace, which is the fruit of active justice for all. However, my longing for a "normal" life must not undermine the service to which God has called me. That would be intolerable. And my service is also to you. That is why I write this letter. I shall surely stand guilty before God if I do not witness against this government.

I think the time has come for your government to make a choice: you are either the "servant of God" of Romans 13, or you are the "beast from the abyss" of Revelation 13. Unless and until the right choice becomes *evident* (through the wholehearted and fundamental change of your policy), Christians in South Africa shall be called upon, *for the sake of their faith*, to resist you as we would the beast of Revelation 13. For the Christian, obedience to God and God's word must be the first priority.

I am aware that the decision to resist the forces of government cannot be an easy one. That is why the synod of the D. R. Mission Church made this so clear last year: "If a Christian is bound by his conscience to follow the way of criticism, which brings him into conflict with the state, then he should obey God more than humans. In this case, however, he must be prepared to accept suffering in the spirit of Christ and his apostles."

Once again, this is not a matter of being brave. Rather, I should like to use this occasion to urge you to realize that peace and salvation, indeed, the future of South Africa, do not lie in more "security laws," in more threats, or in an ever growing defense budget. They lie, rather, in the recognition of the human dignity of all South Africans, in the pursuit of justice, and in respect for the God-given rights of all.

You as whites are not in a position to achieve this on your own. That is why the churches have pleaded for a national convention where the people could be represented by authentic, chosen leadership. We demand the right to have the vote, so that our citizenship in South Africa may become meaningful. Give us the right to express ourselves and our political will. We need to have the opportunity to participate fully and meaningfully in the political processes in South Africa. Is this not the fundamental thing you grant yourself?

I plead that you make use of the offer and the opportunity to have discussions. Honest negotiations with the intention genuinely to share together in South Africa is always better than to stand against each other as enemies.

I am using this letter as an open witness, and thus will make it available to the press.

I thank you for giving me your time.

May God give you wisdom in everything.

Sincerely,
Allan Boesak

Chapter IV

Wholeness through Liberation

"That all may be whole"—these are very beautiful words, not only because they echo so much of what the gospel of Jesus Christ is all about, but also because they echo so much of the African understanding of life. This is indeed a very fitting and gripping theme. We know from the gospel that wholeness of life is life with Jesus Christ; without him, life is somehow just not worth living. Life is somehow empty. Without him, human fulfillment cannot be achieved.

This is the same Jesus Christ who said that he had come so that those who believe in him will not only have life, but will have life in abundance.

Jesus' saying does not mean that we will have material abundance. Material prosperity can deceive us. When we have things in abundance, we hesitate to ask how we got them. We Calvinists all too easily conclude that whatever we have is "a blessing from the Lord." We are so concerned about the question of stewardship that we look at what we have gotten and then ask, How do we spend wisely what we have? We ignore the fact that there is a prior question to that of stewardship—namely, How in the world did we get what we have? A fundamental question, it makes us think about how the world fits together, about why some have what

This address was first given at Calvin College, Grand Rapids, Michigan, Nov. 17, 1980. The text has been edited for inclusion in the present collection.

they have, and others are deprived of what they should have.

When we talk about life in abundance and wholeness, we are not talking about material success, or the power to have our every whim satisfied. We are talking about a life of fulfillment and, I think, such things as friendship and love, life and labor, and the possibility of sharing with others what you have as a human being. I am thinking of wholeness as the fulfillment and recognition of our human-beingness.

So I congratulate you on this theme—it is so rich. I hope that you will be stimulated to make this theme part of the reality of your own lives and of this church that you serve, and part of the reality of the country in which you live.

As for my own country, South Africa, in spite of its material wealth, is a tragic paradigm of brokenness. The wholeness is gone. South Africa today is in the grip of a formidable and sophisticated system, with a stronger economy than ever before and with the price of gold making possible an increase of wealth. Beyond its economic strength, South Africa is probably also the strongest military power on the continent, helped by friendly governments in Europe and the United States that, in spite of weapons and arms embargoes, did in fact go ahead and supply arms to South Africa. This we know from reports published by the United States.

We still have inequality before the law and inequality in both labor and education. Today the government spends two-thirds of the total education budget on white children and one-third of the budget on nonwhite children: something like 650 rand [$550] for a white child, 118 rand [$100] for a so-called colored child, and 49 rand [$42] for a black child per year. We live in a situation where discrimination is still a way of life, enshrined in the laws of the land. In fact, to do what is right and just for persons of another color or ethnic group would probably require that you contravene the law.

Systemic Violence

We still have, in South Africa, a system of racism that is maintained by violence. In the first place there is the systemic violence inherent in apartheid society—the violence that means, for example, that a black man who takes a bride today will be forced tomorrow to leave her behind in some desolate homeland if he finds work in a white city. He will not be able to take her with him without contravening the law, and will see her only for a couple of weeks at the end of the year when he returns for vacation. This systemic violence breaks up black family life. This systemic violence operates in an educational system that, if it allows black children to go to elementary and high school at all, then permits the government to say, "These children cannot go to a white university, because they lack the competence." That is not merely a racist statement, but a statement of fact, because "Bantu" or black African education is so inferior that it does not prepare one for university education. The basic dictum underlying black education in South Africa, as maintained by Dr. Verwoerd in the 1950s, is still true: black children must not get the kind of education that will give them the idea that they can have the same position as white children in South African society.

Violence, in the second place, refers to physical violence as perpetrated by the police and the military in South Africa. The system of white privilege and racism in South Africa, which is known as apartheid, has become a Moloch that needs the blood of children to survive. We saw this in 1976 and again in 1980. When in June of 1980 Capetown blew up, I was working as a minister in that area with young persons and students. For the first time in my life I was in the midst of violence. I saw young persons with nothing in their hands marching in the streets to make clear to the government and the whites of South Africa: "We do not want a heritage of hatred and racism and suspicion and mistrust in South Africa. We want to share with you our anguish for the future of this country we shall inherit, a country where we shall not be safe, where we shall not be able to live as human beings together. Let us change that." And I saw those young persons teargassed; I saw them shot down with rifles.

I have seen so many who want from life nothing more than an opportunity to experience wholeness with wife or husband and children. They do not want wealth or success. All they want is the security of being able to live as human beings. It is denied them. This denial is the violence I am talking about.

In South Africa black humanity still does not count. In fact, the humanity of a black person is not even seen as true humanity. It is against the law for a black woman who must work as a domestic servant in a white city of South Africa to bring her children with her, or to visit them on weekends. Some years ago, somebody asked the minister of Bantu affairs why he did not change this particular law. He said, "You know, we must always remember that these black women are not like our women. They don't want their children with them. They really enjoy being alone and being away from their families." Blacks are viewed as so subhuman that normal human desires cannot be ascribed to us.

Toward the end of 1979 a 12-year-old boy was caught stealing some fruit from a farmer's storeroom. The farmer tied him to a pole, whipped him soundly, and left him for the night. A black evangelist who saw the scene could not take it. He untied the boy in the middle of the night and took him to his parents. The next day, the farmer and his two sons caught the evangelist, tied him up, and beat him to death with sticks and a hose pipe. When they were finally brought before a judge, they were each fined 100 rand [$85]. This is the value attached to black humanity in South Africa today.

We still have an economic system that not only exploits blacks, but requires the destruction of black family life. In a so-called Christian country where much is made of the sacredness of family life, and where a white Dutch Reformed theologian describes the family and the home as the most fundamental and basic unit of faith in the nation, and where there is talk of the sanctity of marriage, it is still a crime for a black man to bring his wife with him to the city where he works, because the cities are white South African territory. He does not belong there; neither do his wife and family. And if he does bring them with him, he will be "harboring an illegal black"; he can go to jail.

The point is not so much that black family life is broken up by the economic system but that the economic system deems migrant labor necessary to its survival. And the migrant labor system makes black family life nothing in the eyes of South Africans. So the question for us is not so much, How do we keep these black families together? Rather, the question is, What do we do with an economic system that necessitates such evils? If this is the price of capitalism, then we need to ask some fundamental questions about that. We still have a system where "security legislation"—legislation meant to "secure" our country, to bring safety to the cities of South Africa—means detention without trial, banning individuals and organizations, exiling some of the best sons and daughters of South Africa, and killing others in South African jails—Steve Biko, to mention only one example among many others.

At this point, I must voice a profound concern about the Reagan administration in the United States of America, which has made it abundantly clear that human rights is not one of its major concerns. Whatever the faults of President Carter, and there may have been many, what he did for the poor, the oppressed, and the struggling in the world of today helped to create a climate in which it was clear that human life could not be taken with impunity and that at least there would be some protest. Even if he did not achieve much in terms of practical programs, that stance of President Carter saved lives. I am concerned for the lives of those who have to struggle against oppressive regimes when those regimes know that human rights will not be a major concern, that the United States will pay closer attention to economic interests.

When will persons in the United States, where so many Christians read and try to understand the gospel, learn that there is no such thing as safety and security and peace where there is not wholeness of life? And when will they learn that if human life is broken in South Africa or Indonesia or El Salvador, there is no way that life can be whole in the United States?

Despite many promises and much talk about change in South Africa, one of the most fundamental aspects of the apartheid policy is still intact. This is the homelands policy whereby only 13 percent of the land is given to more than 80 percent of the population, and whereby, finally and fundamentally, all blacks in South Africa will somehow officially be "endorsed out" of white South Africa. The final goal of the nationalist government of South Africa is that a time will come when there will be no black South African citizens at all. The question will no longer be that of a black majority vis-à-vis a white minority in South Africa, for there will be a number of black minorities scattered all over South Africa. The only majority then will be the white majority. Even though most of the blacks in South Africa will still be living in what is called white South Africa, technically they will belong to some homeland, and they will have no political rights whatsoever in white South Africa. This is the most immoral aspect of the apartheid policy.

But apartheid means even more. It means that the homelands will continue to be a dumping place for our elderly and our youth. It means unemployment, hunger, starvation—injustice. In the homeland area in Kwazulu, a thousand children in one year were admitted to one hospital in one area with kwashiorkor, the most malignant form of malnutrition. When a black child in the homelands contracts measles, that child is 32 times more likely to die from it than is a white child in South Africa.

Where Is the Church?

We are talking about wholeness of life. Desmond Tutu, the secretary general of the South African Council of Churches, tells of speaking to a 10-year-old child on a visit to one of the homelands. "What do you eat?" he asked.

She said, "Sometimes we do not have anything to eat."

He said, "What do you do then?"

"We borrow food from the neighbors."

"If the neighbors don't have any?"

"Oh," she said, "then we drink water to fill our stomachs."

I have seen persons shred newspapers to cook along with their other pieces of food to make a meal, to live, and finally to die of it.

Yet, South Africa wants to be known as a Christian country. And in the midst of all this is the Christian church. What do we do as Christians in South Africa? With regard to the policy of apartheid, the Christian churches can be divided roughly into three groups. There are those who say that apartheid is evil, is irreconcilable with and a denial of the gospel of Jesus Christ, and is, therefore, to be resisted with all our might. Other Christians say that apartheid is an expression of the will of God for South Africa; we find these persons in the white Dutch Reformed churches of South Africa. And there are those, to be found mostly among the English-speaking Christians in South Africa, who view apartheid as a bad thing, but politically the best solution at the moment. It is a question of the lesser of two evils: either the country is overrun by blacks or the apartheid system is used to maintain some kind of equilibrium.

Apartheid is more than an ideology, more than something that has been thought up to form the content of a particular political policy. Apartheid is also a pseudo-gospel. It was born in the church and even today it finds some theological justification in the Afrikaans-speaking Reformed churches. The struggle against apartheid and all that it stands for is, therefore, more than merely a struggle against an evil ideology. It is more than a struggle for the liberation and wholeness of persons, white as well as black, in South Africa. It is also, finally, a struggle for the integrity of the gospel of Jesus Christ. The question is, If the gospel of Jesus Christ can be equated with this system, what is that gospel? This is the crux of the matter.

Our struggle today in South Africa is a struggle for wholeness through liberation. Some of the questions that plague the church in this situation can be reduced to: How does the Christian church react to the violence inherent in apartheid society, and How can the church react to the violence of the police or the military in South Africa? These are questions of more than academic interest.

It is very likely today that you could find, in a racially mixed church, a white parent who wants the preacher to pray for "our boys on the border," thinking of the war on the Namibian border, where the South African military is fighting the guerrillas of the Southwest African People's Organization (SWAPO). In that same church, you would also find a black parent who also wants the preacher to pray for those engaged in the border war, but this black parent has a child who left South Africa in 1976 and joined the guerrillas, because he believes that military struggle is the only way to achieve justice and liberation in South Africa. The church finds itself caught up in this dilemma.

In this context the hypocrisy of white Christians on the issue of violence is incredible. You can hardly expect blacks to believe the gospel of nonviolence coming from those who, all through their history, have relied upon violence and military action to get what they wanted and to maintain unjust systems. Reliance on the "just war" theory was common practice. But now the question of "just revolution," raised by the French Huguenots many years ago (it was not thought up by black revolutionaries), must be faced. What do you do?

The church has not been successful in struggling against racism in society, because it has not yet learned how to deal with it in the church itself, a situation that is not peculiar to the church in South Africa. We are faced with a theological challenge that is at the basis of many other problems. How can the church in South Africa be odedient to God and at the same time be obedient to Caesar?

Conscientious disobedience for the church in South Africa is a reality we can no longer avoid. We know that the church has to offer a prophetic witness to the state. One of the fundamental things about Calvinist Reformed theology is that of prophetic witness. But how do we deal with it if it leads to confrontation with the state? We also know that action is needed; statements no longer suffice. I have seen it happen that the church—that is, the children and parents who worship with me on Sunday—is out there on the streets on Monday protesting for the sake of a humane future for South Africa. At the same time that these blacks are being attacked by police who are ready to kill them, other church members, senior and junior executives in local companies, are sitting in boardrooms drafting statements for the press, to be published Tuesday when everything is over.

So the question is: Where is the church? I have a strong conviction that the church is not in those boardrooms drafting statements. The church is out on the streets. And if the church is on the streets, what does that mean? In the midst of the struggle and in the midst of death, is there *hope*? I think so. And I am not talking about *optimism* about the South African situation. We see how the interests of Western nations are intertwined with the interests of white supremacy in South Africa. We know how the South

African regime would not survive without the active support of Western nations. We see how strong they are militarily, economically, politically. We perceive that in the world at large there is a movement away from what makes for peace and human fulfillment and human wholeness. There is little to be optimistic about.

The difference between optimism and Christian hope is that hope is founded on the fact that even though we were sinners, Jesus Christ came and gave his life for us. And even though he knew what we would do with it, he gave his message to the church, vulnerable though that message may be. The whole point of the parable of the sower is not to say we have to do evangelization, but to point out how vulnerable the word of God is in the world. We have seen that word used to justify slavery and white supremacy, for ideological reasons, for oppression, to keep others down. We have seen that word become a tool in the political games that church persons play. And yet it is the word that has been given us. Therein lies my hope: that the church of Jesus Christ will yet discover the gospel of liberation and hope for human fulfillment and wholeness. The challenge to the church is to discover and implement that gospel: to become whole itself, and to work for the wholeness of life everywhere in the world.

In the nineteenth century a South African walked out of a white-dominated church and formed his own church. His name was Isaiah Shembe. He said to his people:

> My people, you have been told of a god who cannot see you, who has no hands to heal, who has no feet to walk among you. Isaiah Shembe will tell you of a God who has eyes to see you, hands to heal you, feet to walk among you, a God who has love and compassion.

The "experts" of African theology who live in Europe and North America listened and said, "This is a black messiah. For blacks the messiah is always one of their own that they elevate to this idolatrous position." But they were wrong. Shembe was not speaking about himself. He was saying that the god the missionaries preached to Africans in South Africa was a god who could not see them as human beings, could not relate to them, could not touch them, and therefore could not bestow the gift of human wholeness.

In African tradition physical death is but one form of death and not even the worst form. There is another kind of death: you die when others refuse to recognize your human-beingness, when they break up the wholeness of your life. Isaiah Shembe was saying that there is a God who will see you as human beings, who can identify with you. Shembe promised his followers what the god of the missionaries could not give them, because that god was too much the god of whites. This is what Isaiah Shembe shared with his people. This is what I hope that African Christitanity can bring to West Europeans and North Americans.

There is a proverb that you will find in all African languages. I quote it in Sutu: *Motho ke motho ka betho babang*, "I am human only because you are human." My humanity affirms your humanity. Your humanity affirms my humanity. Without that there is no wholeness.

This seems to me to be the gospel truth.

Chapter V

Guarding the Faith: Reflections on the Banning of Black Theology Literature in South Africa

Since the beginning of the 1970s a new theological expression has found articulation in black Christian circles in South Africa. It is called black theology. It caught on like a fire and was accepted by many in the black community as an authentic, meaningful expression of their Christian faith. Articulate black theologians immediately began to put into words the meaning and significance of black theology for black Christians. Yet today, some ten years later, most of the material regarding black theology may no longer be read by South Africans. There is only one book written by a black available, together with a few articles. Apart from that, the only writing on black theology available is the criticism offered by white theologians.

Obviously the government is trying to ban black theology.

Section 1 of the Publications Act 42 of 1974 states that the criteria designed to serve as the basic standards for the censoring of films, publications, and public entertainment are based on "the constant endeavor of the population of South Africa to uphold a Christian view of life." Apart from the fact that some legal ex-

This essay was originally published in *Theology Today* 38 (April-Jan. 1981–82): 182–89. It has been edited for inclusion in this collection.

perts consider the wording of the act "an insult to the art of statutory drafting" (as J. D. van der Vyver put it), there are other questions that must be raised. For instance, can one really speak of a "constant endeavor of the population of the Republic of South Africa," when we are so clearly a multireligious society? And can one speak of the endeavor of the "population" to uphold a "Christian" view of life, as if those who call themselves Christian were Christians, and as if this "endeavor" is the most natural thing in the world for those who live in South Africa?

The most serious question is, What "Christian" view is the government upholding? The view that the most important thing about human beings is their racial classification? That persons can be judged according to the color of their skin instead of the content of their character? That 13 percent of the land can justly be "allotted to" 80 percent of the population, whereas 87 percent goes to whites? That whites, *because of their whiteness*, have the right to decide for everybody else, thereby treating God's human creatures like cattle that can be herded from one part of the country to another? But why go on? Bearing just this much in mind, it is no wonder the South African government wishes to ban black theology.

"Guardian of the Faith"?

The government has made a "study" of black theology. The results can be found in the infamous Schlebusch/Le Grange Report and make incredible reading for anybody who knows anything about black theology. Dr. Manas Buthelezi has written a brilliant reply to that report. Unfortunately, as one might have guessed, I cannot repeat his arguments here for the sake of those who have not read his critique, because it appeared in what is now a banned publication.

But another point must be made. In banning something of a theological nature the South African government makes a *theological* judgment. Theology has to do with one's faith and how that faith finds expression in one's daily life. If that faith is threatened, one tries to protect it. In banning black theology, the government has taken upon itself to be the "guardian of the faith."

We are confronted with the pretension that the government knows the true faith, accepts it, lives by it, and resolves to protect it. We know that this is a belief highly acclaimed in classic Reformed confessional documents and that the government also has the duty to guard the faith as well as to protect the faithful. One must remember, however, that this is a point of view formulated at a time when church and state, sword and word, were almost indistinguishable, and when the ideal of a theocracy was kept very much alive. The situation is quite different today, and most Reformed churches have ceased to hold their governments to that duty in the sense in which it was originally meant.

Evidently, however, the government in South Africa does see itself in such a role. It considers itself a Christian government, a proper channel to "further the aims of the Kingdom and to withstand the powers of the Anti-Christ," as the Belgic Confession says. But the question remains: Dare a government, which through its policies and practices so clearly deviates from scripture, whose laws are so blatantly unjust that its purported Christianity is a blasphemous mockery, take upon itself the role of "guardian of the faith"? Surely it must be obvious that a government that persecutes the faithful cannot at the same time be the protector of the faith? The Bible contains not only Romans 13 (how government ought to be); it also includes Revelation 13—how government ought *not* to be. The servant of God can very easily become the beast. This is one of the things black theology wants to make clear.

In order to understand this point even better we must take a brief look at what the government of South Africa is trying to ban. Banning something means that it is considered "undesirable." It does not contribute to better mutual understanding and better interpersonal relationships. As writing, black theology is considered "inciting," "undermining the good order of public life" and the authority of the government. It constitutes a threat to the "Christian view" of life. Therefore, it has to be done away with.

What is black theology, then? Black theology is the attempt of black Christians to understand and interpret their situation in the light of the gospel of Jesus Christ. They want to do this in such a way that the black community understands that the gospel is commensurate with the achievement of black humanity.

The situation in which blacks live is a situation of oppression. Blacks are disenfranchised and have no rights recognized by law. They are considered unequal, and they live under laws that have robbed them of their dignity and self-respect. The gospel, however, is a gospel of liberation. Therefore, black theology is a theology of liberation. It believes that Christianity is not a "white religion," an instrument for the effective oppression of blacks. It believes that God is a God of justice and liberation, always choosing the side of the weak and the downtrodden. It believes that God has taken sides in the South African situation and calls upon blacks to join in the struggle against inhumanity and injustice.

The "why" of black theology is not difficult to understand. Until now, white Western Christian theology lived under the illusion that it was a *universal* theology, speaking for all those who called themselves Christian. Christian theology had been cast into a white Western mold, reflecting the beliefs of the rich and the powerful as prescribed by their position of wealth, comfort, and power. It did not reflect the cries and the faith of the nonwhite poor and oppressed. The anxieties of the slaves of white Christians, the fears of indigenous peoples decimated by whites in order to take over their land, the despair of those who were kept in economic and political servitude by the systems imposed by white Christians—the plight of these unfortunates was not even considered in Christian theology. Christian theology had become a white theology, an ideology justifying the privileged position of those in power, rather than the critical sword of the gospel revealing the truth of God's mercy and justice.

Black theology also calls itself a "contextual" theology: it functions, and wants to be understood, within a particular situation. In South Africa, the context of black theology is the life experience of blacks in South Africa—an experience shaped by the realities of a system called apartheid. Therefore it deals with apartheid, pass laws, racial discrimination, poverty, oppressive "security" laws, economic exploitation, and all the other bitter realities of being black in South Africa.

Black theology also has to deal with the questions arising out of this situation: What does it mean to be black in South Africa? What does it mean to live in a world controlled by white racists? What if one believes in Jesus Christ as Lord and these others also call themselves Christians? What if they say they believe in the same Bible, even deriving from it the arguments they use for the destruction of your humanity?

We now begin to have an inkling of what might be moving the government when it bans books on black theology. In dealing with their situation, black theologians have been as frank and honest as one dares to be in South Africa. The themes of oppression, liberation, and anger ring out like a bell in every discussion.

But there is more. Black theology also speaks of the discovery of being a human being. As a theology, it is not merely a reflection on a situation or an experience. It is not a political ideology. It deals with black realities *in the light of*, and under the critique of, the word of God. Of course, this means that the situation will be judged severely, but it also means that black theology itself falls under the judgment of the word. It deals with suffering and hope, with love and peace, with reconciliation and justice, with oppression and liberation from oppression. Its demands are clear for whites, but they are just as clear for blacks.

Once again, black theology is the expression of the faith of black Christians. It says that in spite of white manipulation (slavery, "sons of Ham," the theology of apartheid), the gospel is still God's liberating word. It says that the covenant God of the Torah and the prophets cannot be *possessed*, least of all by oppressors. God cannot be overcome, least of all by the pharaohs, the Baals, and the Dagons of this world.

Black theology is not the *only* theological expression in the world, but in my opinion it is the only authentic way for blacks to pursue their Christian faith. It gives hope, restores faith, kindles joy, and brings life again.

This is what the government wants to ban.

Black theology is indeed a ringing, honest, and absolutely necessary indictment of white Christianity in South Africa. It is a burning flame of legitimate anger at what is being done in the name of the God whose very name spells liberation, compassion, justice, love. Yet at the same time black theology offers reconciliation and peace in a situation where citizens do not trust each other, where we have been driven apart by laws, and where we are kept apart by fear and hatred. It speaks of Christian hope where so many have lost all hope.

It is true that whites have difficulty with the concept of reconciliation and love in black theology. Black theology clearly says that reconciliation does not mean to gloss over what is wrong, to hide evil, and to harmonize what cannot stand side by side. It does not mean taking hands and singing "black and white together." For black theology, reconciliation means confronting evil, unmasking sin, and coming together through the sharing of sorrow, repentance, suffering, and death. Christian love is not a matter of feeling good but of doing what is right. Black theology offers liberation, not only to blacks but also to whites, telling them that they will never be free from their fear until blacks are free from bondage; telling them that in Christ the walls of partition have been broken down and the true Christian view is that of a country where all its citizens live in peace—together. It is not the peace that is the containment of violence or merely the absence of war (civil war?), but the peace that is the active presence of justice.

Ananias Mpanzi has said that although black theology directs its voice to blacks, it hopes that whites will also hear and be saved.

This is what the government wants to ban.

In this kind of faith lies the salvation of South Africa. This is the kind of faith South Africa needs to save us from the idolatry of a civil religion that carries within itself the seeds of self-destruction. A government that will not face the truth about itself is totalitarian and incapable of being saved. It legitimizes a false consciousness and a pseudo-innocence in the minds of the people, thereby piling up the stones that kill the prophets.

By banning the truth, it bans not only prophetic judgment but also the possibility of repentance and conversion. It prevents the people from understanding "the things that make for peace"; it is in fact persecuting Christians because of their faith. It becomes an adversary of the liberating and reconciling work of God in the world, an enemy of the gospel of Jesus Christ. It is foolish bravery to try to block the God of justice.

Ask the pharaoh.

It must be made clear that black theology, as an expression of faith, cannot be banned. Of course the South African government can ban books and articles. It can ban the persons who wrote them. But it cannot take away the faith of an oppressed people, the discovery that God always has been, and is now, on the side of the poor and the needy. It cannot take away the truth that this God is passionately involved in history for the sake of the lowly. It cannot take away the message of liberation that the Bible brings and it cannot dilute the call that is inherent in biblical proclamation—the call to participate with God in the struggle for the kingdom and its justice in the world.

This is not to say that white Christians have not tried to do so. God knows *how* they have tried! They have tried to manipulate the biblical message; they have tried to make of God a tribal, white God; they have tried to spiritualize the dynamic power of the gospel, almost succeeding in making it the opiate of the people. But—and this may rightly be called a miracle—God has once again proven to be God. God's word cannot be bound.

One must admit that there has been a measure of "success" for the government. Its actions against black theology have made it easy for South African churches, so deeply imbued with the sin of racism, to avoid the challenge of black theology and to resist its impact. What the government has done has also made it easy for the churches to avoid meeting the challenge of black consciousness. The result is that a theology relevant to the needs and the struggle of blacks is operative only in "pockets" of concerned and prophetic Christians—vulnerable, frowned upon by church leadership, and wide open to intimidation by civil authorities.

The theology that should have been gratefully received by the whole of the church, accepted by the church as a gift from God, is still seen as undermining "official" theology. Many in the churches regard black theology as at worst communist-inspired and politically subversive, and at best as some sort of a guerrilla theology. I am not thinking only of those churches that regard themselves as "white" churches, and I am not speaking only of whites in the church. I am also thinking of black Christians. For so many of them, government action against black theology and black theologians has brought fear and anxiety so that once more blacks have found it expedient to flee with nervous enthusiasm into the false sanctuaries of an anemic, pietistic, pie-in-the-sky-when-you-die theology to prove to church leaders (and the government?) that they are not "political" but "evangelical." Once again, the false dichotomy between the "spiritual" and the "worldly" (read: political) gospel is being extolled as virtuous and this heathen way of life is praised in churches already over anxious not to disturb the existing order.

So the South African churches will take that much longer to come to grips with the realities of the South African situation. It will take us that much longer to completely understand our role and responsibility in the struggle for liberation.

To understand and accept black consciousness in the Christian church in South Africa is not merely to understand the necessity of genuine black leadership in a given historical moment. Black consciousness entails a new understanding of oneself, of one's situation, and of the dynamics of struggle. It means coming to grips with the realities, limitations, and possibilities of one's own situation.

With regard to the church, this would mean that the church in South Africa would no longer have an inflated opinion of itself, but understand its role as servant in the world. It would understand its own identity as a church and its identification with either the oppressed or the oppressor. Once it has succeeded in overcoming its fear, it would ultimately, by God's grace, become an authentic agent of liberation and reconciliation in a torn and sorrowfully divided society.

I sincerely believe that black theology would have been able, in its small way, to help the church in understanding all this. Born in the communities of the poor and the oppressed, black theology could have helped to bring the church closer to the people it hopes to serve. Now it is still largely hidden from our eyes. All this I would consider the most tangible result and at once the tragic success of government action against black theology.

But I must repeat: no government can ban black theology. It cannot ban it, because it cannot really ban the faith of a people. That is why the truth for which black theology stands will increasingly be authenticated in the lives and witness of black Christians in South Africa. It wins hearts and minds because it is authentic and life-giving. It convinces because it is, in the true sense of the word, gospel truth. If it poses a threat to the present system in South Africa, it does so because the gospel, proclaimed honestly and in obedience to Christ, is always a threat to that which is wrong. It forms a threat because the way of life this government wants to protect is in many respects the antithesis of the demands of the gospel. It forms a threat because loyalty to Christ the Lord is superior to loyalty to Caesar.

Imagine, God Forbid . . .

Dorothee Sölle tells a story from Soviet Russia that explains very well why the authorities are waging their war on black theology in South Africa. An old lady, forgetting that she was within earshot of a local party secretary, said to her friend: "Thank God, it looks like rain."

Disturbed, the party man said: "But you must know by now, Comrade, that you cannot say that. God does not exist."

"Ah, yes, Comrade," replied the old lady, "I understand that. But imagine, God forbid, that there *is* a God!"

South African government officials, along with many others, know that there is a God. But their God is white—or colorless, which is the same thing. Their God blesses their laws and gives them the authority to make even more such laws. Their God blesses their guns, and gives them more money for their gold so they can buy even more guns. The eyes of their God are closed to the injustices they perpetuate.

Black theology talks about a God who sides with the oppressed. God listens to their cry; their suffering becomes God's suffering. God identifies with them. God's power is proved (ask the pharaoh!); God's promise is true. God will deliver the needy and helpless:

God, give your own justice to the king,
  your own righteousness to the royal son,
so that he may rule your people rightly
  and your poor with justice.

Let the mountains and hills
  bring a message of peace for the people.
Uprightly he will defend the poorest,
he will save the children of those in need,
  and crush their oppressors. . . .

He will free the poor man who calls to him,
  and those who need help,
he will have pity on the poor and feeble,
  and save the lives of those in need;
he will redeem their lives from exploitation and outrage,
  their lives will be precious in his sight. . . .

Blessed be his name forever. . . .
May every race in the world be blessed in him,
  and all the nations call him blessed!

Blessed be Yahweh, the God of Israel,
who alone performs these marvels!
Blessed forever be his glorious name,
may the whole world be filled with his glory!
  Amen. Amen! [Ps. 72, Jerusalem Bible].

". . . Imagine—God forbid!—that there is *such* a God!"

Chapter VI

Holding on to the Vision

And the Lord answered me:
  Write the vision;
  make it plain upon tablets,
  so he may run who reads it.
For still the vision awaits its time;
  it hastens to the end—it will not lie.
If it seem slow, wait for it;
  it will surely come, it will not delay.
Behold, he whose soul is not upright in him
    shall fail,
  but the righteous shall live by his faith
[Hab. 2:2–4].

Six hundred years ago, in July 1381, John Ball stood on Blackheath Common in London, England, and spoke to a vast crowd. The crowd consisted of the poor, the dejected, the empty-handed populace of England, those with "no name in the streets," who long had been oppressed by the rich and the powerful.

As John Ball spoke, he inspired his hearers to listen, to believe, and for one glorious moment to throw off their despair and hope-

This sermon was preached on the 600th anniversary commemorating the Peasants' Revolt (1381), Blackheath Common, London, England, June 6, 1981. The text has been edited for inclusion in the present collection.

lessness, to stand up and challenge the seemingly unshakable order of their world.

How did John Ball do it? He shared this vision: of a day when they would all be recognized as human beings created in the image of God, of a day when England would no longer know masters or serfs, of a day when the goods of God's earth would be shared by all. "Matters shall not be well in England," he said, "until all things are held in common." He spoke, and, beyond their present realities and darkness, the poor and the oppressed saw and understood God's possibilities for this world. John Ball truly was a prophet, for the vision of the prophet is rooted always in the cry of the poor and oppressed: a cry that moves the heart of God.

The book of the prophet Habakkuk begins with the cry: "How long, Lord?" Habakkuk's world was one of injustice, destruction, and violence. "The law is slacked"—it favors the wicked, denies the right of the weak, and perverts justice. Those whose "own strength is their god" were those who seemed to control the world in which Habakkuk lived. They loved not, they cared naught save for their own self-interest, which they defended with relentless oppressive violence. They "live in luxury." Their "food is rich." They "devour the righteous." They "unsheathe the sword every day to slaughter the nations without pity."

This situation spurs the prophet's cry: "How long, Lord?" It is a cry of deep anguish and endless pain, a cry of dark and helpless despair. It is a cry for love and compassion, a cry for justice.

That great theologian of the Reformation, John Calvin, says of this passage:

> Tyrants and their cruelty cannot be endured without great weariness and sorrow; for indignity on account of evil deeds kindles within the breasts of all, so that they become wearied when they see that wicked men are not soon restrained. Hence almost the whole world sounds forth these words, How long, how long? When anyone disturbs the whole world by his ambition and avarice, or everywhere commits plunders, or oppresses miserable nations, when he distresses the innocent, all cry out, How long? And this cry, proceeding as it does from the feeling of nature and the dic-

> tate of justice, is at length heard by the Lord. For how comes it that all, being touched with weariness, cry out, How long? except that they know that this confusion of order and justice is not to be endured? *And this feeling, is it not implanted in us by the Lord? It is then the same as though God heard himself, when he hears the cries and groanings of those who cannot bear injustice.*[1]

In this situation what does the prophet do? He does not despair. He does not resign himself to the situation. He does not caution the people to accept things "because that's the way it is." He knows only too well that is *not* the way it should be. The prophet, rather, turns to the God who awakens the desire for justice in the heart of the oppressed, who hears a self-description in their cries: "I will take my stand to watch." There is certainty here, a sure faith that cannot be shaken, even by the destructive, violent powers that rule the world. For the vision must come; it must become the reality of the world.

The prophet's vision tells him that the "world" that the powerful have structured is a lie, a rejection and denial of the world that God created. The vision insists that the powers of evil that control and manipulate this "world" are *not* invincible. They can be challenged. The vision reveals that liberation from oppression and the realization of human fulfillment for the poor are not empty dreams. They can become reality. The vision is rooted in history and in the God of history.

The prophet's vision is a vision of the God of the exodus who could not remain unmoved by the pain and suffering of the people. God took sides—*for* the oppressed people and *against* the power and military might of the pharaoh.

The prophet's vision is a vision rooted in the God who uprightly defends the poor, who saves the children of those in need, who liberates the oppressed but crushes the oppressor (Ps. 72). It is a vision rooted in the God who "breaks the bow of the strong soldier, but gives strength to the weak . . . lifts the poor from the dust, and raises the needy from their misery" (1 Sam. 2:4, 8).

The God of the prophet's vision is the God of the Jubilee, who proclaims that only a radical and fundamental challenge to false political, social, and economic relationships in Israel is acceptable (Lev. 25), the God of the prophets who knew that the Lord expects us to do justice and love mercy (Mic. 6:8), the God of Jesus Christ, the promised one, who is the embodiment of the kingdom of the poor and who came to proclaim the acceptable year of the Lord.

The vision of the prophet is a vision of liberation: to be saved from oppression, despair, and the humiliation of perpetual poverty; to be redeemed from the need to crawl and lie in order to stay alive; to be released from the fear of freedom and from the mad desire to be like the rich. The vision of the prophet rejects the false security of slavery and accepts with faith and joy the promise of a new life. The vision of the prophet accepts the truth of one's own humanity and, most of all, calls only the living God "Lord."

The vision of the prophet does not conform to the patterns of this world. It does not revolve around glory and world domination. Nor does it find inspiration in the accumulation of wealth and the power of destructiveness. It, rather, finds its meaning in the lives of the poor and the oppressed, the weak and the downtrodden. The vision of the prophet is realized in the signs of the kingdom of God: in the lame who walk, the lepers who are cleansed, the blind who see again, and the poor who hear the good news preached to them (Matt. 11)—in the wonderful things that happen to the lowly visited by God.

It is this vision that inspires priests and nuns as they join the people of El Salvador, Nicaragua, Guatemala, and Chile as well as in many other places where the struggle against injustice, oppression, and inhumanity continues. It is this vision that inspires the young in South Africa to face dogs, tear gas, detentions without trial, and gunfire for the sake of liberation and human fulfillment. It is this vision that inspires the oppressed everywhere in an environment of poverty, fear, informers, torture, imprisonment, and death. The realization of the vision may seem slow. The vision, however, is not deceptive. It will be realized. Its realization cannot be delayed.

Habakkuk reminds us that this vision is threatened by the high and mighty. It is threatened by those whose "soul is puffed up in them," by those who, in boundless arrogance, think that their positions of power are unshakable. They who threaten the prophet's vision have always been in the world. We find their stories in the scriptures: the pharaoh, for example, who asked with disdain and contempt: "Who is the Lord, that I should listen to his voice?" (Exod. 5). They always are very sure of themselves, very confident of their power. The powerful who threaten the realization of the prophet's vision are with us today, also—those, for example, who build their empires on the backs of the poor; those who create and perpetuate an economic system that has made the continuation of dependency and poverty the very basis of its survival; those who place a higher value on ideology than on human dignity; those who export the madness of militarism to maintain the growth of their own economies.

There are others today who also threaten the realization of the prophet's vision: those who refuse to become involved because they fear the loss of their privilege; those good Christians who believe they can remain neutral as the poor and the innocent are sacrificed on the modern altars of Moloch and Mammon; those who do not yet understand that neutrality is no longer possible, that it is in fact the worst kind of partiality there is—taking the side of the oppressor without assuming responsibility for the oppression. These persons threaten the prophet's vision because the vision threatens their way of life, their power, their wealth, their precious pseudo-innocence, the "world" that they have created and that pushes to the edge of the abyss the world that God created.

What correlation is there between the vision of the prophet and the church, the body of Christ, the bride of the Lord, the witness to the kingdom of God? The church is called to proclaim this kingdom with its justice, love, peace, and wholeness. The church is called at all times and under all circumstances to follow in the footsteps of the Lord whose kingdom it proclaims.

The church can do nothing other than be on the side of the poor and the dispossessed. It cannot but proclaim a message of liberation from misery, oppression, poverty, domination, exploitation, fear. That means it cannot but search and fight with all its might for justice, peace, reconciliation, human fulfillment. It has no choice but to be the light of the world and the salt of the earth.

In 1381 the English peasants faced a church that did none of this. The peasants faced a church that made common cause with the rich and the powerful and made an unholy pact with the nobility and the military. In denying God's lowly, by reason of its coalition with the nobility and the military, the English church in 1381 also denied its Lord.

We must ask if this really was the church. Was not John Ball, the poor, rebel priest who provided hope for the poor and inspired the peasants in their struggles, the true image of the church of Jesus Christ? Was not Bartolomé de Las Casas the true image of the church of Jesus Christ when he was the only one to preach against slavery, even when the whole Catholic Church was providing biblical justification for it, and sharing in the profits with the perpetrators of that inhuman institution? Was not Martin Luther King, Jr., the true image of the church when he dared to dream of love, peace, justice, and human understanding, even as the authors of hatred and bigotry were plotting to kill the dreamer?

Is the white Dutch Reformed Church in South Africa the true image of the church of Jesus Christ? The Dutch Reformed Church is the spiritual resting place of oppressors and assures them on Sunday that whatever they have done during the week was for the sake of "Western Christian civilization" and done in the name of Christ. Is not the true church, rather, the assemblage of those who in the name of Christ resist apartheid, who side with the poor and the oppressed, who are harassed, detained, tortured, and banned?

The church of Jesus Christ must have the courage and the obedience to join with God in the struggle throughout history for the sake of justice. If the church does not participate in this struggle, the commemoration today of the Peasants' Revolt in 1381 will be nothing more than empty mockery. We dare not stand here celebrating the bravery of the peasants in 1381 if we are not willing to participate in the struggle for the sake of the poor *today*. We dare not commemorate their struggle for justice if we are not consumed by a desire for justice today. We dare not honor the memory of John Ball today if as a church we are not willing to be as prophetic today as he was in 1381.

How shall the church participate in the struggle today for the sake of the poor? "The righteous shall live by his faith" (Hab. 2:4b). This is not the kind of faith that has been doled out to the poor over and over again: an irresponsible, other-worldly religiosity that dared to call itself "faith." No, this is the faith of the prophet, a faith rooted in the history of Yahweh and Yahweh's people. This is the faith that is rooted in the gospel of liberation and in the Messiah, the one promised by God. This faith refuses to accept the world as it is; it has a vision of a new world. It refuses to accept with resignation the present situation. This faith will work ceaselessly for the coming of the new age that was inaugurated in Jesus the Messiah. This faith will not bow down to fear, for fear silences, blinds, paralyzes. This faith clings to the vision of a world in which human dignity will be respected, in which God's material gifts will be shared by all, in which fellowship will be universal, in which reconciliation even with our torturers will become a reality.

This is the faith of Jeremiah who could see the truth about the false gods who claimed God's world and God's people for themselves: "Their idols are like scarecrows in a cucumber field. . . . They cannot do you harm, neither is it in them to do good" (Jer. 10:5).

This is the faith of Archbishop Oscar Romero:

> The hope that the church fosters is a call . . . to the poor that they take responsibility for their own future, that they conscientize themselves, that they organize. . . . The call is one of support for their just causes and demands. It is the poor who force us to understand what is really taking place. . . . Our persecution is nothing more nor less than sharing in the destiny of the poor. The poor are the body of Christ today. Through them he lives on in history. . . . If they kill me, I shall rise again in the Salvadoran people.

This is the faith that in the midst of oppression, hunger, fear, death, and utter despair will yet shout—and if it cannot shout, it will whisper:

> For I am assured that neither death, nor life, nor angels, nor principalities, nor things present, nor things to come, nor powers, nor height, nor depth, nor anything else in all creation, will be able to separate us from the love of God in Jesus Christ our Lord.

God bless you. Amen.

Chapter VII

Liberation and the Churches of Africa: "To Break Every Yoke"

This year, the churches of Africa will assemble under the theme: "Following the Light of Jesus Christ." For Africa, this theme cannot be a simplistic expression of joyful innocence or a triumphalistic war cry. Rather, let it reveal the pain, the sorrow, the suffering, and the fragile, hopeful faith of captive peoples. For Africa is a wounded continent, and the wounds have not yet healed.

Colonialism has been exchanged for newer, subtler forms of economic exploitation in which underdevelopment and dependency are both real and inescapable. Famine, hunger, and starvation still claim their victims by the millions, and the truth is that these very often are not economic problems; they are *political* problems.

Africa is torn by conflict and war. This is so partly because the continent has become the "testing ground" for the ideologues of the superpowers, the battlefield for their mad desire to rule the world. But it is also true that Africa knows too many iron-fisted rulers who have no respect for human rights. The colonial governor's mansion is now occupied by the representatives of new

This address was delivered at the All Africa Conference of Churches' General Assembly held in Nairobi, Kenya, Aug. 2–12, 1981.

power elites that have as little concern for the people as did the colonialists. All too often "independence" has not meant a new, meaningful life for the people, or a return to the values of African life that would have revitalized society. Values such as the wholeness of life, the meaning of human-beingness, and the relationship between human beings and nature have not been resuscitated in African life, because these values tend to subvert the economic interests of the new elites and their neocolonialist masters.

Oppression and political uncertainty have driven many countries into the arms of the madness called militarism. Many African countries spend more on armaments than they do on food, education, and human development.

In South Africa racism still reigns supreme, and oppression and dehumanization continue unabated. The violence inherent in the system of apartheid, systemic and otherwise, continues to escalate, and the murder of children in 1976 and 1980 has brought tension to the breaking point. What makes this situation unique is not so much the existing oppression as the fact that all of this is done by Christians, in the name of Jesus Christ, as explicit as it is blasphemous.

The African churches are meeting here in the midst of struggles for liberation and human fulfillment, against oppressive ideologies and systems of domination; amid growing tensions within and between nations; in short, against the evil powers and principalities resisting God's kingdom in the world. The theme "Following the Light of Jesus Christ" will therefore have to echo the cry of the poor, the dejected, the cry of the children of Africa who, like those in South Africa, are giving their lives in the struggle for liberation and God-given humanity. This theme will have to echo the cry of the 4.5 million African refugees; the cry of those whose oppression and dehumanized condition have become a perpetual darkness.

The God of the Bible

If the church wishes to be heard at all in Africa, we shall have to proclaim the Lord of the scriptures. That Lord is the God of the exodus, who could not remain unmoved by the plight of the people. God *saw* their oppression. God *heard* their cry and liberated them from slavery, from meaninglessness and alienation, to the fulfillment of their humanity in the service of the living God. God took sides—*for* the oppressed people, *against* the power and military might of the pharaoh. God shared the condition of an oppressed people; a slave people became the people of God. God's name was written across its history. It was claimed by God; it no longer had to suffer under the illusion that it was the property of the pharaoh. God's love was proven through mighty deeds so that Israel might come to understand that the power of the pharaoh was a pseudo-power, and that in the presence of the living God the pharaoh was a false god whose very inability to do justice was an exposure of his preposterous claims.

The exodus revealed to the Israelites the will and nature of the God who called them into being. It was this act that formed the basis for understanding God's will throughout history. It was the exodus that gave Israel the certainity that this God is one who uprightly defends the poor, who saves the children of those in need, who liberates the oppressed but crushes the oppressor (Ps. 72). When Hannah sang her song of praise it was based on historical experience with this living God: "He breaks the bow of the strong soldier, but he gives strength to the weak. . . . he lifts the poor from the dust, and raises the needy from their misery" (1 Sam. 2:4, 8).

The prophets knew beyond any shade of doubt what the Lord wanted of them—to do justice, to love mercy, and to walk humbly with God (Micah 6:8). The prophets knew what it meant to know the Lord:

> Woe to him who builds his house by unrighteousness,
>   and his upper rooms by injustice;
> who makes his neighbor serve him for nothing,
>   and does not give him his wages;
> who says, "I will build myself a great house
>   with spacious upper rooms,"
> and cuts out windows for it,
>   paneling it with cedar,
>   and painting it with vermillion.

Do you think you are a king
  because you compete in cedar?
Did not your father eat and drink
  and do justice and righteousness?
  Then it was well with him.
He judged the cause of the poor and needy;
  then it was well.
Is not this to know me?
  says the Lord [Jer. 22:13–16].

The God of the Bible is the God of Jesus Christ who took upon himself the condition of oppression and poverty. Jesus Christ sides with the poor and the weak. He speaks of himself as a "servant." Jesus becomes one of the *'am ha-aretz,* the poor of the land. He is a man without majesty, a man of sorrows and familiar with suffering, whose life reflects so much of the life of oppressed peoples today.

But still his name is Yoshua: liberator. He brought the message and reality of hope and liberation. His life was an example of divine radicality, a profound disturbance of the existing order. He was revolutionary in that he offered an alternative consciousness to the sterile ideological postures of the Zealots, the Sadducees, the Pharisees, and the Essenes. Let us not be distracted by useless debates about Jesus and the Zealots, as if his revolutionary presence were dependent on his being a Zealot. The Zealots' goal was to expel the Romans from Palestinian soil in order to reestablish the law in all its purity and to reestablish the politico-religious institutions of Israel. Jesus' revolutionary projection went beyond the dream of recovering a nationalistic, politico-religious kingdom whose very core was a legalism that he denounced as oppressive. Indeed, he did not come to save a legal system. He came for the sake of poor, oppressed, blind, weak persons: the lowly who had no value at all except insofar as they were useful to the power elites. Jesus, however, taught the oppressed, the *'am ha-aretz,* that God loved them, and that they were of far greater value than the flowers of the field and the birds of heaven, which Solomon in all his glory could not equal.

Jesus defended the lowly against the religious tyranny of high priests and scribes: the Sabbath is made for man, not man for the Sabbath; the law is the liberating servant to humanity. He profoundly challenged the worldly power of political authorities both Jewish and Roman, and through his presence brought the demands of his kingdom into our history.

This Jesus is Lord. It is he who died and arose from the dead. To him is given all power in heaven and on earth. His claim upon our lives is, therefore, as total as his liberation is total. There is not a single area of life, not a single moment of our human history, that is not claimed by the lordship of Christ. The demands of his kingdom—justice, love, and peace—address the totality of our human existence.

This is the Christ whose light illuminates our darkness. His message of liberation is the message of the church in the world. This is the message the church in Africa must proclaim if it is to be authentic. It is the message of the God of the Bible: what God did for the people of Israel, God can do again today. It is a message that he who came to proclaim the acceptable year of the Lord is still the head of his church.

The liberation the church proclaims is total. It is liberation from sin in all its manifestations of alienation from God and neighbor. It is liberation from economic exploitation, dehumanization, and oppression. It is liberation from meaninglessness and self-alienation, from poverty and suffering. It is liberation toward a meaningful human existence seeking freedom and human fulfillment. It is liberation for the service of the living God, so that God's people will no longer be subjected to the tyranny of false gods.

For the churches this liberation involves joining the struggle against political oppression and economic exploitation; against racism and all forms of human degradation; against the destruction of human-beingness wherever it may occur on the continent. Let me repeat here what I have said elsewhere: joining the struggle for human liberation in Africa does not mean christianizing the struggle, "taking over" as it were, what others have been doing long before. But it does mean taking responsibility for the historical reality into which the kingdom of God has entered. It does mean being a Christian presence in the midst of that struggle, keeping alive and witnessing to the goals of the kingdom of God for our world.

It means keeping alive, in the midst of the struggle, God's possibilities. It means being the embodiment of God's demands for love, justice, reconciliation, and shalom for the world that has been reconciled with God in Jesus Christ. In all this the church should be guided, not by fear, resignation, or any ideology, but by its desire to be true to the gospel of its Lord. The church should understand that it must take sides just as its Lord took sides with those "who had no helper." Neutrality is not possible; and in any case, it is the worst kind of partiality there is: taking the side of the oppressor without taking responsibility for it.

It may very well be that the churches of Africa are totally unfit for this task. Indeed, the church in Africa itself is in need of liberation. The church in Africa is still plagued by a colonial mentality; we have not truly become a church *for Africa*. We have accepted church structures that are alien to Africa, that simply cannot respond to the needs of the people as they should. We cling to theologies that fail to speak to the people of Africa. Throwing aside African values, such as the wholeness of life, we uncritically accept sterile Western debates, and we proudly call ourselves "Evangelicals" or "Ecumenicals." African churches all too often still cling to a pietistic, other-worldly religiosity that has no bearing on the present situation in the world. In doing this we not only deny the lordship of Christ, but forget that this is the kind of theology that justified our slavery and oppression right through history to the present. The church in Africa needs liberation in order to become an authentic healing agent of God in the world.

Healing is the process of working toward peace, wholeness, community, reconciliation. It is a demanding ministry, and in our torn and wounded continent it will be an extraordinarily difficult task. But it must be done. Being the church of Jesus Christ means taking up the ministry of healing.

There are a few things I suggest that we remember as we take up this awesome responsibility.

First of all, healing presupposes brokenness and hurt. To recognize the hurt and brokenness in African churches and nations means to identify the causes of that brokenness. It means understanding that brokenness in terms of political, economic, and social realities as well as in terms of human alienation and suffering. Moreover, it means not trying to gloss over these realities even when it may be "expedient" not to name both the sin *and* the sinner.

Secondly, healing asks for the kind of solidarity with victims that does not come through formal acceptance of a creed, but through sharing of the pain, by taking upon oneself the hurt of the others. Healing includes the understanding that the church accepts and recognizes the presence of Christ himself in the brokenness of humankind. The God of the Bible is not a dispassionate, unmoved mover who engages in self-contemplation. Neither is God detached, aloof from human struggles, suffering, and pain. No, as much as God is "grieved to the heart" by human evil (Gen. 6:6), so is God stirred and moved by human suffering: "In all their afflictions, he was afflicted" (Isa. 63:9a). Nowhere does this become clearer than in the life and death of Jesus the Messiah. In the face of human suffering, Jesus is, as Kosuke Koyama so correctly stated, the "brokenhearted God." Out of his brokenheartedness over the condition of human brokenness comes his judgment, his infinite compassion, his justice, his shalom.

This at once opens a third perspective: it is the brokenhearted God, the suffering Servant of the lord, who heals. In other words, true healing comes through the willingness to suffer, to take upon oneself the brokenness of the other. It is the giving up of life that brings new life. To hold onto life at all costs will mean to lose it.

In this context a question emerges clearly: Will the churches of Africa be able to do all this? I am convinced that it is possible if we allow the liberating God to begin liberation in the church. It is possible if the churches of Africa take the gospel seriously and if we begin to apply the demands of the kingdom of God to all areas of life. This will mean that we must be serious about getting rid of theologies that have colonized our minds, so that our proclamation of the church can be relevant to the Africa in which God has placed us *today*. It will mean that we will more than ever cling to the confession of the lordship of Jesus Christ and refuse to bow down to the ideologies that try to threaten, intimidate, or seduce the church of Jesus Christ. It will mean that our love for Jesus Christ will not become an excuse to emigrate out of history but, rather, a commitment to him *in* history: a commitment to challenge, to shape, to change, to subvert, and to humanize human history until it conforms to the terms of the kingdom of God.

False Gods and Their Idols

Finally, the liberation of the church requires the ability to discern the difference between false gods and the living God. The world is full of powers and principalities that claim for themselves divine power, and claim from human beings an obedience and allegiance that Christians can and must give only to God. These powers become gods when we follow them blindly and put our trust in them. In our modern world, I believe that racism, nationalism, militarism, and materialism have become such idols.

False gods not only challenge the living God; they effectuate an *exchange*.[1] "You have exchanged the glory of God for the image of an ox that eats grass" (Ps. 106:20). This is what happens in that incredible story in Exodus 32 where Israel exchanges Yahweh for the golden calf. There the exchange is complete. The worship of the living God is exchanged for the worship of a deaf, dumb, lifeless beast. The history of Yahweh with the people, the history of a mighty liberation, is exchanged for a false consciousness that both denies Israel's past and distorts its present and its future: "These, O Israel, are your gods which led you out of the land of Egypt" (v. 8). Israel exchanges the liberated consciousness of a free people for the slave mentality of the Israelites prior to Yahweh's great liberating act—the exodus.

The exchange goes further. The Bible is persistent in its teaching that idols are dead. Jeremiah says that an idol is "a tree one cuts down from the forest," which is then beautified with silver and gold, and clothed in violet and purple. Idols are merely the handiwork of an artisan. They cannot speak. They cannot walk. They cannot see. They cannot do justice, defend the widow and fatherless, deliver the poor and needy out of the hand of the wicked. They know not, neither will they understand (Ps. 82).

When we bow down before these idols and accept their power, we lose this discernment and, with it, our responsibility and our true humanity. When we believe that these false gods can, in fact, walk, *we* become lame. When we believe *they* can see, *we* become blind. When we believe *they* can speak, *we* become dumb. When we believe that *they* know, we exchange *our* understanding for the instruction of idols, which is a delusion, empty foolishness (Jer. 10:3, 8).

The church of Jesus Christ is called to be particularly sensitive to false gods. It must be a liberated church, able to identify the false gods in our society and to call them what they in fact are. It must be a liberated church, well aware that the false gods of the age are pseudo-powers that have already been exposed by the crucified Christ so that they can be challenged. It must be a liberated church that confesses amid all the signs of the false gods' destructive madness: "Their idols are like scarecrows in a cucumber field. They do not speak; they have to be carried, for they cannot walk. Do not fear them for they cannot do harm, and they lack the power to do good" (Jer. 10:5).

"Not like these is the portion of Jacob" concludes Jeremiah (v. 16). Indeed God is not. God is the liberator God of the exodus, of the prophets, and of the Messiah. God is the liberator God of those who today call upon the name of God and proclaim God's lordship.

Chapter VIII

You Are a True Son of South Africa: An Open Letter to Bishop Desmond Tutu

My dear Desmond,

Everybody is again talking about you, especially the government. And again they talk in the only language they seem to know when addressing us: the language of accusation, threats, and intimidation. But you and I know this is really the violent verbosity of deeply fearful men.

Apparently taking away your passport was not enough. Making the work of the South African Council of Churches infinitely more difficult did not suffice. We are now hearing the so-familiar sounds that are the prelude to *kragdadigheid* [“resoluteness,” “powerful efficacy”], boding ill for you and the Council. You are, they say, “supporting subversive elements,” “encouraging a revolutionary climate in South Africa,” and now “promoting the aims of the ANC” [African National Congress].

Because of all this you are now considered an enemy of the state, indeed of South Africa, a dangerous subversive who does not “deserve” a passport and now even runs a greater risk—or so we have heard. After having made you the victim of a campaign promise to appease the worst of the racists, they now want

This letter first appeared in the South African newspaper *Argus* on Sept. 16, 1981. Bishop Tutu wrote a response, which appears here after the text of the open letter.

to use you to divert attention from their obvious inability to face the consequences of their disastrous policies and to undo the damage done to our country and its people after decades of apartheid.

My first reaction was anger. Precisely who is the danger to our society and to the future of this country? Who has caused the problems that now plague South Africa? Who has taken away the few pitiful political rights we had so that they could inflict their policies upon us without responsibility *to* us? Whose laws are making criminals out of men, women, and children who want only a decent life together as a family?

Not by any stretch of the imagination can you be accused of "creating a revolutionary climate" in South Africa. No, it is your very accusers, who through their intransigence and their stubborn refusal to respect the dignity of black personhood, who are doing that. It is they who deny us meaningful participation, insult us with the puppet institutions they themselves would have scorned. It is they who through draconian measures have set aside the rule of law, banned organizations that wanted peaceful change, detained without trial, banned and exiled the best of the sons and daughters of South Africa.

It is they who have done so much to help convince generations of black South Africans that nonviolent protest has no chance in South Africa. For years we have petitioned, marched, pleaded, cried, tried to speak to the conscience of the white South African government. They have answered with police, with detentions and tear gas, with dogs and guns. And with that infinite contempt of those who have nothing left but the power of the gun.

No, it is not you who have turned so many of our older persons into creatures without hope and joy, and so many of our younger persons into desperados. It is they.

But then again, I thought, if only they knew you, the man who earned the love and respect of the world. I heard you speak so often, here and abroad, with such honesty. I have seen you cry tears of genuine anguish as you spoke of the unwillingness of whites to listen and to understand. You want so much to believe in the residue of goodness in whites that many of us think you naive. I have seen how your desire for true reconciliation between black and white has earned you the scorn of those who do not allow themselves to think in such terms.

For them you are an enemy of South Africa. For us you are a true South African, a champion of the cause of the poor, the weak, the dispossessed, a follower of Jesus Christ. You have done no more than to reflect the deep feelings of the black community. You have been the voice of the voiceless.

You have a deep love of your country. But they will never understand that. For them, loving South Africa means accepting apartheid and white supremacy, humiliation and exploitation. It means to bow your head in submission and say *Ja baas* ["Yes, boss"] even if deep in your heart you despise yourself.

They do not understand that loving South Africa means precisely to despise apartheid and all that system has made of all of us, white and black. It is to fight for a country where we shall no longer be ruled by fear and greed. But you speak a truth that is too humbling, a message that is too disturbing.

It is true that prophets are not honored or loved in their own land, but a nation that cannot respond to such a love has set fire to its own future.

So let them accuse you; millions of us love and support you. When the true history of this country comes to be written, you will be counted as a true son who fought for its integrity and its life. Let them accuse you; in the church of Christ you shall be honored as a pastor and a prophet whose obedience to God surmounted fear of those who rule this world.

As for myself, I thank God I may call you friend and brother. Let us pray for one another, so that the temptation to succumb to false gods shall not overcome us, and that our vision of the promised land shall not be dimmed or distorted. And let us be assured that neither death, nor life, nor angels, nor principalities, nor things present, nor things to come, nor powers, nor height, nor depth, nor anything else in all creation will be able to separate us from the love of God that is in Christ Jesus our Lord.

Response

September 22, 1981
The Rev. Dr. Allan Boesak
Hoek Street 6,
Bellville South, 7530

My dear Friend,

I am not sure that an open letter is ever responded to, inasmuch as it frequently is a literary device to call attention to the author's points of view. Whatever the convention on these matters, I want to place on record my deep appreciation for your courageous and heartwarming action.

It would have caught all kinds of headlines if you had said you were repudiating me. It is fashionable in certain quarters to gain credibility with the powers that be and the white elite by vilifying me. You would have become the blue-eyed boy of the establishment. I am, therefore, all the more grateful that you decided to go against that particular grain. Consequently, your letter has in fact not received much publicity, certainly nothing in the Transvaal that I know of. We fight against all kinds of principalities, as you are well aware. I think I will send it to the *Sowetan,* who might be moved to publish it; then it might see the light of day in these parts.[1]

Be that as it may, I just want you to know how much I am indebted to you for what you have done. Thank you. God bless you richly.

Yours sincerely,
Bishop Desmond Tutu

Chapter IX

Black and Reformed: Contradiction or Challenge?

The Reformed tradition in South Africa is more than three hundred years old. It was brought here by Dutch Calvinists, who were followed by French Huguenots, and still later by Scottish Presbyterians and Swiss missionaries. When our Khoi ancestors were confronted with Christianity for the first time, it was the reformed expression of it that they experienced. It was this tradition that was to have a lasting impact on the history of South Africa and on the lives of all its citizens. When our ancestors accepted Christianity three centuries ago, they became the members of a reformed church.

Yet this history is racked with contradictions. The Europeans who claimed this land, who scattered and killed its people, did it in the name of a Christian God whom they prayed to as Reformed Christians. When they introduced slavery and enforced it with the most vicious forms of dehumanization and violence, it was the Bible read through Reformed eyes and arguments from the Reformed tradition that gave them justification for such acts of violence and human tragedy. The God of the Reformed tradition was the God of slavery, fear, persecution, and death. Yet, for

This address was presented at the first conference of the Alliance of Black Reformed Christians in Southern Africa (ABRECSA), Hammanskraal, Oct. 26, 1981. The text has been edited for inclusion in the present collection.

those black Christians this was the God to whom they had to turn for comfort, for justice, for peace.

It was of Reformed Christians that a Dutch pastor of the nineteenth century spoke when he wrote:

> How is it possible that there could be any religious or, let me say, human feeling in persons who force their servants, mostly children of blacks shot dead, to sleep outside without any protection whatsoever in these cold nights, so that these unhappy wretches cover themselves with ashes, thereby inflicting upon themselves terrible burns. . . ? How can there be any religious or even human feeling in persons—big strong men—who beat these children mercilessly with whips at the slightest provocation, or even without any reason at all. . . ? God knows, and I myself know, what indescribable injustices occur in these parts! What gruesome ill-treatment, oppression, murder![1]

And yet these were persons who were supposed to be brothers and sisters in Christ, persons who were supposed to form with others the one body of Christ in his church—the Reformed Church.

The contradictions did not disappear as time went on. On the contrary, they multiplied. Today, three hundred years later, black Reformed Christians come together to ask the question: What does it mean to be black and Reformed in South Africa today? It is a question that not only concerns our past. It also concerns our present and it has a direct and fundamental bearing on our future. Indeed, one can also put the question in another way: Does the Reformed tradition have a future in South Africa?

Apartheid: Heritage of the Reformed Tradition

Today, no less than three centuries ago, being both black and Reformed is an expression of a painful paradox. Reformed Christians have the power in this country, as they did three hundred years ago. Now, as then, they call themselves Christians, and they proudly announce that they stand within the Reformed tradition.

Through the power of the gun and sheer trickery they have claimed for themselves 87 percent of this land and they call it "white South Africa." Their avarice and boundless greed have claimed the vast resources and riches of this country. The wealth with which God has blessed this land, the breathtaking natural beauty that is the work of divine artistry, the majestic mountains, the sea, the fertile valleys—on all this is carved out in brazen arrogance: "For whites only." Blacks have come to understand that even though the Bible teaches us that the earth is the Lord's and the fullness thereof, experience has taught us that here the earth belongs to whites.

These Reformed Christians have created a political, economic, and social dispensation that they call apartheid. It is based on racism and white supremacy, on economic exploitation and the misuse of political power. They have made laws that are a perversion of justice and offer no protection for the poor, the weak and defenseless millions of our land against the power of their oppressors. For the sake of economic privileges that they regard as their right, they deliberately put asunder what God has joined together. They despise the sanctity of marriage and family life when it comes to blacks. They treat the homeless with a callousness and brutality that stun the mind. They detain without trial. They silence the prophetic voices of the nation through arbitrary bannings. They terrorize the innocent. They are prepared to kill children in order to maintain apartheid and white supremacy.

Apartheid is unique. But its uniqueness does not lie in the inherent violence of the system, or in the inevitable brutality without which the system cannot survive, or in the dehumanization and the contempt for black personhood, or even in the tragic alienations and the incredible costs in terms of human dignity and human relationships. No, the uniqueness of apartheid lies in the fact that this system claims to be *based on Christian principles.* It is justified on the basis of the gospel of Jesus Christ. It is in the name of the liberator God and Jesus Christ, the Son of God, that apartheid is perpetuated, and it is Reformed Christians who are responsible for it. Apartheid was born out of the Reformed tradition; it is, in a very real sense, the brainchild of the Dutch Reformed churches. It is Reformed Christians who have split the church on the basis of race and color, and who now claim that racially divided churches are a true Reformed understanding of the nature of the Christian church.

It is Reformed Christians who have spent years working out the details of apartheid, as a church policy and as a political policy. It is Reformed Christians who have presented this policy to the Afrikaner as the only possible solution, as an expression of the will of God for South Africa, and as being in accord with the gospel and the Reformed tradition. It is Reformed Christians who have created Afrikaner nationalism, equating the Reformed tradition and Afrikaner ideals with the ideals of the kingdom of God. It is they who have devised the theology of apartheid, deliberately distorting the gospel to suit their racist aspirations. They present this policy as a pseudo-gospel that can be the salvation of all South Africans.

In this uniqueness lies the shame of the Christian church in this country. Apartheid is the grave of the dignity and the credibility of the Reformed tradition.

Today we have reached a state of affairs where many, especially blacks, have come to believe that racism is an inevitable fruit of the Reformed tradition. In the experience of millions of blacks this tradition is responsible for political oppression, economic exploitation, unbridled capitalism, social discrimination, and the total disregard for human dignity that have become the hallmark of South African society.

By the same token, being Reformed is equated with total, uncritical acceptance of the status quo, sinful silence in the face of human suffering, and manipulation of the word of God in order to justify oppression. Being Reformed is to support the intransigence of our present rulers and to expect the unconditional submission of the oppressed.

The anomaly has become more acute than ever. For black Reformed Christians who suffer much under the totalitarian rule of white Reformed Christians, the question is fundamental and decisive. We have reached a point in our history where we can no longer avoid it. Black and Reformed: is this a burden that has to be cast off as soon as possible, or is it a challenge toward the renewal of church and society? Does the Reformed tradition have a future in South Africa?

A Reform in Need of Reform

But we must ask a prior question. Is the Afrikaner version of the Reformed tradition the whole truth? Is the equation between being Reformed and being oppressive and racist justified? In this country, as Douglas Bax has shown, Reformed theology has in many instances become a curious mixture of pietism, German Romanticism and *Volkstheologie,* and the negative aspects of Kuyperianism. Is this acceptable? Is the justification of tyranny Reformed?

Of course, in trying to answer all these questions I must of necessity be brief and selective. My aim here cannot be to give a detailed exposé of Reformed doctrine, but rather to highlight those aspects of the tradition that are especially relevant to us in our situation, and that need to be redeemed from the quagmire of political ideology and nationalistic propaganda to which they have fallen victim in South Africa.

The first thing that I should mention, then, is the principle of the supremacy of the word of God. In the Reformed tradition it is the word of God that gives life to our words. It is the word of God that shapes life and provides the church with a basis on which to stand. Scripture is the indisputable foundation of the life and witness of the church in the world and it is the guiding principle for all our actions.

Manipulation of the word of God to suit culture, prejudices, or ideology is alien to the Reformed tradition. But the way in which Reformed Christians in this country have used the Bible to justify black oppression and white privilege, the way in which the gospel has been bypassed in establishing racially divided churches, the way in which scripture has been used to produce a nationalistic, racist ideology, is the very denial of the Reformed belief in the supremacy of scripture. The word of God is the word that gives life. It cannot at the same time be the justification of the death that comes through oppression and inhumanity. It is the word that speaks to our total human condition and offers salvation that is total, complete. For us today this means that, although the Bible is not a handbook for politics or economics, it nonetheless reveals all we need to know about God's will for the whole of human existence, including the spiritual, political, economic, and social well-being. The church believes that the Bible provides us with the fundamental principles of justice, love, and peace that we in the making of our societies ignore or deny at our own peril. It is this word of God that is the critique of all human actions and that holds before us the norms of the kingdom of God.

The kingdom of God is inextricably bound up with the lordship of Jesus Christ—another precious principle for those who adhere to the Reformed tradition. Christ is Lord of all life, even in those situations where his lordship is not readily recognized by wilful humans. We believe passionately with Abraham Kuyper that there is not a single inch of life that does not fall under the lordship of Christ. All of life is indivisible, just as God is indivisible, and in all of life—personal and public, politics and economics, sports and art, science and liturgy—the Reformed Christian seeks the lordship of Christ.

Here the Reformed tradition comes so close to the African idea of the wholeness of life that these two should combine to renew the thrust that was brought to Christian life by the followers of Calvin. Reformed piety was *never* intended to include withdrawal from the world. The admonitions of politicians and even (Reformed!) churches to black Christians to "keep out of politics" are not only unbiblical; they are also, as Max Warren called them, the "essence of paganism." He quotes a missionary from Uganda:

> Without realizing it . . . we have drifted back into the old polytheism against which the prophets of the Lord waged their great warfare. The real essence of paganism is that it divides the various concerns of a man's life into compartments. There is one god of the soil; there is another god of the desert. The god of wisdom is quite different from the god of wine. If a man wants to marry he prays at one temple; if he wants to make war, he must take his sacrifice elsewhere.

> All this is precisely where the modern paganism of our secular society has brought us today. Certain portions of our life we call religious. Then we are Christians. We use a special language. . . . We call that our Christianity—and there we stop.
>
> We turn to another department of our life called politics. Now we think in quite different terms. Our liturgy is the catchwords of the daily press. Our divine revelation is the nine o'clock news. Our creed is "I believe in democracy." Our incentive is the fear of—we're not sure what. But it certainly is not the fear of the Lord.[2]

This kind of religion is far from the faith that characterized Reformed Christians from the very beginning. Their faith said that Christians were responsible for their world. Their Christianity was what Calvin College philosopher Nick Wolterstorff has called, "world-formative Christianity." As Reformed Christians we see ourselves as human beings who are responsible for the world in which we find ourselves. It is a world made by us, and we are capable of making it different. More than that: we *should* make it different. It *needs* reform. Furthermore, the exercise of that responsibility is part of the discipleship to which the Lord Jesus Christ has called us. It is not an addition to this discipleship, but an integral part of it. Doing what we can to reform the social world in which we live is part of our spiritual life.[3]

For us as black Reformed Christians that means that in the following of Jesus Christ the spiritual experience is never separated from the liberation struggle. In the heart of this process God is experienced as a Father to whom every effort and every struggle is offered. Our worship of God is what must give direction and content to our action in the world. From God come bravery and courage, truth and justice. Because God raised our Messiah from the dead to demonstrate the truth of his word, God will also give life to those who, in the path of Jesus, give their lives for others.

In South Africa, white Reformed theology has persistently pointed out that we live in the "broken reality" of a fallen world. This is true. But in the theology of apartheid this leads to the acceptance, the idealization, and institutionalization of that brokenness, and of that kind of apathy that induces Christians to accept sinful realities such as racism.

In true Reformed theology, however, the recognition of the broken, sinful realities of our world becomes the impulse toward reformation and healing. It means we understand that human beings do not automatically seek the glory of God and the good of their neighbor. That is why it becomes a Christian's task to work actively for the good of one's neighbor. In a fallen world, the structures that we create are tainted by sin and will not automatically have a liberating, humanizing effect on human lives. They will therefore have to be changed so that they may serve the humanization of our world. This means that Reformed Christians are called on not to accept the sinful realities of the world. Rather we are called to challenge, to shape, to subvert, and to humanize history until it conforms to the norm of the kingdom of God.

Social Justice: The Reformed Tradition

What shall we say about the equation of South African oppressive society and the Reformed tradition? It is necessary that we once again refute the blasphemous claim that apartheid is Christian. We must understand that the Christian character of a government is not proven by good intentions, or by the number of times it shouts Lord, Lord! It is proven by the care of the poor, the protection of the weak and the needy, the suppression of evil, the punishment of oppressors, the equitable distribution of wealth, power, privileges, and responsibilities. As Calvin says: "the Lord recommends to us . . . that we may, insofar as everyone's resources admit, afford help to the needy, *so that there may not be some in affluence, and others in need.*"[4]

It is tragic that the reformer's concern for social justice is not reflected in the policies of all those who claim spiritual kinship with him. South African history might have been different if white Reformed Christians in South Africa had taken his word on human solidarity seriously: "The name neighbor extends indiscriminately to every man, because the whole human race is united by a sacred bond of fellowship. . . . To make any person our neighbor, it is enough that he be a man."[5]

In the area of social justice, Reformed belief was expressed magnificently by Abraham Kuyper speaking to the Christian Social Congress in 1891:

> When rich and poor stand opposed to each other, Jesus never takes his place with the wealthier, but always stands with the poorer. He is born in a stable; and while foxes have holes and birds have nests, the Son of Man has nowhere to lay his head. . . . Both the Christ, and also just as much his disciples after him as the prophets before him, invariably took sides *against* those who were powerful and living in luxury, and *for* the suffering and oppressed.[6]

Unlike so many rich Calvinists and other Christians who keep on telling the poor that poverty is the will of God, Kuyper refused to believe it:

> God has not willed that one should drudge hard and yet have not bread for himself and his family. And still less has God willed that any man with hands to work and a will to work should suffer hunger or be reduced to the beggar's staff just because there is no work. If we have food and clothing then it is true the holy apostle demands that we should therewith be content. But *it can neither nor may ever be* excused in us that, while our Father in heaven wills with divine kindness that an abundance of food comes forth from the ground, through our guilt this rich bounty should be divided so unequally that while one is surfeited with bread, another goes with empty stomach to his pallet, and sometimes must even go without a pallet.[7]

Later, another Reformed theologian, Karl Barth, put it in these words:

> The human righteousness required by God and established in obedience—the righteousness which according to Amos 5:24 should pour down as a mighty stream—has necessarily the character of a vindication of right in favor of the threat-

> ened innocent, the oppressed poor, widows, orphans, and aliens. For this reason, in the relations and events in the life of people, God always takes his stand unconditionally and passionately on this side and on this side alone: against the lofty and on behalf of the lowly; against those who already enjoy right and privilege and on behalf of those who are denied and deprived of it.[8]

It is in vain that the oppressive system of apartheid and its defenders claim any Reformed legitimation. Rather, the Reformed tradition calls for resistance to so blatantly an unjust government as is the South African.

Government: The Reformed Tradition

For Reformed Christians, government is not "naturally" an enemy. We believe with Calvin that governments are instituted by God for the just and legitimate administration of the world. But note two things. First, the expectation that government is not the enemy of the people must not be read as blind acceptance of any kind of government, but is in fact a crucial criterion for judging the actions of a government. Secondly, God institutes the authority of government for the *just* and *legitimate* administration of the world. A government, then, in order to be able to claim this divine institution and in order to be legitimate, has to respond positively to the expectation that scripture has of it: it is to be a shepherd of the people (Ezek. 34).

In terms of any modern concept of democracy, as well as in terms of Calvin's understanding of legitimacy, the South African goverment is neither just nor legitimate. For the Reformed tradition, a government should be obeyed because it has the authority instituted by God. But there is always one very important proviso: we obey government *insofar* as its laws and instructions are not in conflict with the word of God. Obedience to earthly authority is only obedience *in God*. On this point John Calvin is clear:

> But in that obedience which we have shown to be due to the authority of rulers, we are always to make this exception,

> indeed to observe it as primary, that such obedience is never to lead us away from obedience to him to whose will the desires of all kings ought to be subject, to whose decrees all their commands ought to yield, to whose majesty their scepters ought to be submitted. And how absurd would it be that in satisfying men you should incur the displeasure of him for whose sake you obey men themselves! The Lord, therefore, is King of Kings, who when he has opened his sacred mouth, must alone be heard, before all and above all men; next to him we are subject to those men who are in authority over us, but only in him. If they command anything against him, let it go unesteemed. And here let us not be concerned about all that dignity which the magistrates [government] possess; for no harm is done to it when it is humbled before that singular and truly supreme power of God.[9]

And Calvin ends with an exhortation to courage and obedience, reminding us that "we have been redeemed by Christ at so great a price as our redemption cost him, so that we should not enslave ourselves to the wicked desire of men—much less be subject to their impiety."[10] Therefore the call is: "We must obey God rather than man."

This was the spirit caught by the Scottish reformation when it formulated article 14 of the *Confessio Scotica:*

> [It is our duty] to honor father, mother, princes, rulers, and superior powers: to love them, to support them, yes, to obey their charges *unless repugnant to the Word of God*. To save the lives of the innocent, to repress tyranny, to defend the oppressed.[11]

Commenting on article 25 of the Scottish Confession, Karl Barth says:

> We can afford the state such positive cooperation only when the signficance of the state as *service of God* is made clear and credible to us by the state itself, by its attitude and acts,

> its intervening on behalf of justice, peace, and freedom, and its conduct toward the church. That is the condition which the *Confessio Scotica* is right in constantly laying down. If that condition is not fulfilled, those who administer it make a mockery [of the service of God]. But in that case we can take no share in their responsibility, we cannot further their intentions, we cannot wish to strive with them to attain their aims. We cannot do it under any conditions or on any pretext.[12]

So when Beyers Naudé sides with the poor and the oppressed in South Africa *he* is the true representative of the Reformed tradition, not those who banned him and sought to bring dishonor to his name.

When the Presbyterian Church of Southern Africa decided to challenge the government on as fundamental an issue as Christian marriage, it is closer to the Reformed tradition than are those who vindicate an unjust law.

It is not the perpetrators of injustice, but those who resist it, who are the true representatives of the Reformed tradition.

Exigencies of a Black, Reformed Future

Black Christians who are Reformed have no reason to be ashamed of this tradition. Of course, this is not to say that Reformed Christians have not made mistakes. We know only too well the tendency of those who adhere to this tradition to become self-righteous. We have often exhibited an arrogance that becomes self-sufficiency and gives rise to a tendency toward isolationism, because we feel we do not need anybody else. Think of how the doctrine of election has been used to foster a false sense of superiority and how often it was coupled with nationalism. Indeed, it is, as Wolterstorff says:

> Sometimes one is [instead] confronted with that most insufferable of all people, the triumphalist Calvinist, the one who believes that the revolution instituting the Holy Common-

> wealth has already occurred and that the social order has been reformed sufficiently for its roles to serve nicely as instruments of obedience for the committed ones. Of these triumphalist Calvinists the United States and Holland have provided plenty of examples. South Africa today provides them in their purest form.[13]

It is my conviction that the reformed tradition has a future in this country only if black Reformed Christians are willing to take it up, make it truly their own, and let this tradition once again become what it once was: a champion of the cause of the poor and the oppressed, clinging to the confession of the lordship of Christ and to the supremacy of the word of God. It will have a future when we show an evangelical openness toward the world and toward the worldwide church so that we shall be able to search with others for the attainment of the goals of the kingdom of God in South Africa. I do not mean that we should accept everything in our tradition uncritically, for I indeed believe that black Christians should formulate a Reformed confession for our time and situation in our own words.

Beginning with our own South African situation, we should accept our special responsibility to salvage this tradition from the grip of the mighty and the powerful who have so shamelessly perverted it for their own ends and let it speak once again for God's oppressed and suffering peoples. It is important to declare apartheid to be irreconcilable with the gospel of Jesus Christ, a sin that has to be combatted on every level of our lives, a denial of the Reformed tradition, a heresy that is to the everlasting shame of the church of Jesus Christ in the world.

To accept the Reformed confession is more than a formal acknowledgment of doctrine. Churches accepting that confession thereby commit themselves to show through their daily witness and service that the gospel has indeed empowered them to live in this world as the people of God. They also commit themselves to accept in their worship and at the table of the Lord the brothers and sisters who accept and proclaim the lordship of Christ in all areas of life, and to work ceaselessly for that justice, love, and shalom that are fundamental to the kingdom of God and the kingly rule of his Son. Confessional subscription should lead to concrete manifestation in unity of worship and cooperation in the common tasks of the church. In South Africa adherence to the Reformed tradition should be a commitment to combat the evil of apartheid in every area of our lives and to seek liberation, peace, justice, reconciliation, and wholeness for all of God's children in this torn and beloved land.

We must be clear. It is one thing when the rules and laws of unjust and oppressive governments make it impossible for the church to carry out its divine task. But it is quite another thing when churches purposely reject this unity and this struggle, as the white Reformed churches of South Africa have consistently done. Apartheid is not simply a political ideology. Its very existence has depended and still depends on a theological justification by these same white Reformed churches. This, too, is part of our task: in struggling *against* apartheid, we struggle *for* liberation; *against* an oppressive and inhuman ideology, but also *for* the sake of the gospel and the integrity of the church of Jesus Christ. Christians and churches purporting to serve the gospel by the justification of apartheid on biblical grounds do so only at the risk of blasphemy.

I am also convinced that in this struggle some Reformed expressions of faith, now centuries old, and for many redundant, can provide us with both prophetic clarity and pastoral comfort. Lord's Day I of the Heidelberg Catechism asks the question: "What is your only comfort in life and death?" The answer is:

> That I, with body and soul, both in life and death, am not my own, but belong to my faithful Savior Jesus Christ; who with his precious blood has fully satisfied for all my sins, and delivered me from all the power of the devil, and so preserves me that without the will of my heavenly Father not a hair can fall from my head; yea, that all things must be subservient to my salvation, wherefore by his Holy Spirit he also assures me of eternal life, and makes me heartily willing and ready, henceforth, to live unto him.

This is one of the most powerful statements of faith I have ever encountered. In our situation, when black personhood is thoroughly undermined, when our God-given human dignity is being trampled underfoot, when our elderly are uprooted and thrown into the utter desolation of resettlement camps, when even the meager shelter of a plastic sheet is brutally taken away and mothers and their babies are being exposed to the merciless winter of the Cape, when young children are terrorized in the early hours of the morning, when the prophetic voices of our youth are teargassed into silence, when the blood of our children flows in the streets of our townships—what *then* is our comfort in life and in death? When we are completely at the mercy of those for whom our humanity does not exist, when our powerlessness against their ruthless rule becomes a pain we can no longer bear, when the stench of our decaying hope chokes us half to death, when the broken lives and silent tears of our aged show the endlessness of our struggle, when the power of the oppressor is arrogantly flaunted in the face of all the world—what *then* is our comfort in life and death? That I, with body and soul, both in life and death, am not my own, but belong unto my faithful Savior, who is Jesus the Liberator; Christ the Messiah and *Kyrios*, the Lord.

Is this excessive spiritualization? No, it is not. But it is a revolutionary spirituality without which our being Christian in the world is not complete, and without which the temptations that are part and parcel of the liberation struggle will prove too much for us. Furthermore, in the situation in which we find ourselves, it is of vital importance that we be able to resist the totalitarian claims of the powers that rule South Africa so harshly. The most frightening aspect of apartheid is the totality of control that the government seeks to exercise over human lives—from the subtle and not so subtle propaganda to the harsh, draconian laws designed to ensure the "security" of the country. Apartheid is a false god whose authoritarian audacity allows no room for the essence of meaningful humanity: freedom under God. It is of vital importance that we never forget to whom our ultimate allegiance and obedience are due.

In this country, the government will come to expect more and more unquestioning submission for the sake of "national security." More and more the government will expect the church to participate in its "total strategy." Such participation could only take the form of theological justification of the national security ideology, the sanctification of the militarization of our society, and the motivation of South African soldiers for the "holy war" against communism.[14] The church will be expected to applaud the kind of theology expounded by the state president at the centenary celebrations of the Nederduitse Gereformeerde Sendingkerk in October 1981: "The total onslaught against South Africa is a total onslaught against the kingdom of God."

Furthermore, as the situation of violence and counterviolence develops and the fear of whites that they will lose their overprivileged position grows, the courage of those who seek justice will be challenged.

So the confession that Jesus Christ is Lord of my life is not spiritual escapism. It is a confession with profound implications for the whole of life. It is a fundamental theological affirmation of the place of the Christian in this world, and it firmly sets the limits of the powers of this world. It places us within the best tradition of the Christian church through the ages, opening our eyes and ears to the inspiration of the "great cloud of witnesses on every side of us." It is a reminder, in the midst of the struggle, that our lives have meaning only when they are in the hands of the one who has given his life for the sake of all others. And although he is the Lamb who is slaughtered, for those who call him Lord he is also "Jesus Christ, the faithful witness, the firstborn from the dead, the ruler of the kings of the earth" (Rev. 1:5).

It is comfort, but it is more: it is the quiet, subversive piety that is quite indispensable for authentic Christian participation in the struggle for liberation. And in this struggle I am inspired by the words of the Belgic Confession:

> The faithful and elect shall be crowned with glory and honor; and the Son of God will confess their names before God his Father and his elect angels; all tears shall be wiped

from their eyes; *and their cause, which is now condemned by many judges and magistrates as heretical and impious, will then be known to be the cause of the Son of God.*[15]

This, also, is our tradition and is worth fighting for.

Chapter X

God Made Us All, But . . . Racism and the World Alliance of Reformed Churches

Since its meeting in Nairobi in 1970, the World Alliance of Reformed Churches has not really given much attention to the issue of racism. Granted, it may have taken a deliberately low profile on this matter because of its desire to support the World Council of Churches in its efforts to combat racism. Or it may have wanted to give its member churches ample opportunity to give such support. It may have argued that duplication of such efforts was not necessary. Be this as it may, I am convinced that the time has come for the World Alliance to take a firm stand on the issue of racism, a stand that is its own, based on its concern for and solidarity with those churches within its fellowship that suffer under racism, and based on its own understanding of the gospel and the Reformed tradition.

There are a number of reasons why I believe that the World Alliance of Reformed Churches should assume a more active role in the struggle against racism:

1) Black thinker and activist W.E.B. Dubois has been proven absolutely correct in his prediction that one of *the* problems of the twentieth century would be the race problem.

This address was delivered at the meeting of the World Alliance of Reformed Churches in Ottawa, Ontario, Canada, August 1982.

2) The admirable work of the World Council of Churches in this regard for the last ten years or more has shown beyond doubt the insidious and extremely dangerous nature of racism.

3) Moreover, instead of abating, racism has grown. Christians in western Europe have become increasingly aware of the problem there, and in the United States racism in numerous ways has once more taken on a cloak of respectability.

4) Racism has taken on new, subtler forms and has found powerful allies in such ideologies as militarism, nationalism, and the doctrine of national security.

5) In the political field, it seems that "liberal politics" has come to the end of its solutions and its energies. In the United States, for example, the impasse is painful, and the general reaction of many liberals is to "outconserve" the conservatives. The responsibility of the church in such a situation, is, now more than ever before, to challenge not only the myopic theologized patriotism of yet another brand of "evangelicalism," but to proclaim the vision of the kingdom of God that transcends the narrow boundaries of race and nationalism and brings justice to the poor and oppressed.

6) A last reason lies in the reality of the situation of the Republic of South Africa itself. Not only is South Africa the most blatantly racist country in the world, but it is also the country where the church is most openly identified with the racism and oppression that exist in that society.

In 1980, black South African Christians made a statement in which this painful realization was put on record:

> The churches to which we belong have conformed to the patterns of a racist society. The persistent cries of the black people that the church is not consistent with the demands of the gospel of Jesus Christ have fallen on deaf ears.[1]

Although this was said of *all* churches in South Africa, it remains true that the white Dutch Reformed churches must assume special responsibility for the situation. At the same time, the work of the World Council of Churches has not directly influenced these churches and the only truly ecumenical family that remains to utter the direct prophetic word is the World Alliance of Reformed Churches.

Something else, however, must be said. Although black Christians in South Africa are almost unanimous in their acclaim and support of the actions of the World Council of Churches and to a lesser extent those of the Lutheran World Federation, the three million blacks in the member churches of the World Alliance of Reformed Churches remain painfully uncertain about the stand of their own confessional family. This is all the more pressing inasmuch as it is the Reformed tradition that had been so effectively and ruthlessly used to justify black oppression and white racism in South Africa.

All this is of singular importance, for the struggle in South Africa is not merely against an evil ideology; it is against a pseudo-religious ideology that was born in and continues to be justified out of the bosom of the Reformed churches. The consequences of this for the future of the Christian church in South Africa are staggering, for ultimately, beyond denomination and tradition, the credibility of the gospel of Jesus Christ is at stake.

Racism: Structured Sinfulness

It is not my intention here to join the current debate about the "right" definition of racism. Even as this debate goes on, oppression and racial discrimination, dehumanization and suffering, exploitation and rejection continue. The cries of anguish of the rejected children of God are far more articulate, and the suffering and pain far more real, than correct definitions will allow.

Yet, we must have some idea of what we are talking about, if only to give our discussion some direction.

First of all, racism is an ideology of racial domination that incorporates beliefs in the cultural or inherent biological inferiority of a particular ethnos. It uses such beliefs to justify and prescribe unequal treatment of that group. In other words, racism is not merely attitudinal, but structural. It is not merely a vague feeling of racial superiority, but a system of *domination,* furnished with social, political, and economic structures of domination. To put it another way, racism excludes groups on the basis of race or color. It is, first, exclusion on the basis of skin color or ethnicity, but exclusion is then cemented into place for the purpose of assuring subjugation. It is in this light that the current "changes" in South African racial policies must be understood. The government, instead of bringing about fundamental changes that would secure meaningful participation in society—peace and well-being for all—is only introducing certain concessions that will do no more than allow a select group of blacks to have limited economic benefits and limited political participation under white control. The overall effect is not to bring justice to all, but to strengthen white supremacy. Here the church is called to be particularly watchful and sensitive so that we acquire the ability to ask questions of a fundamental nature.

Secondly, racism has not always been with us. It came in the wake of European colonization. It became an essential part of a historical process of cultural, economic, political, and psychological domination, and it continues to manifest itself in all these areas. Racism became essential to what Helmut Gollwitzer has called the "capitalistic revolution": "the revolution of the white, Christian, Protestant peoples that would spread all over the world to open the era of slavery which even today (albeit not in the same form) is not yet ended."[2] It is clear that racism cannot be understood in individual, personal terms only. It must be understood in its historical perspective and in its structural manifestations.

Thirdly, however true these observations may be, Christians must say more. Racism is sin. It denies the creatureliness of others. It denies the truth that all human beings are made in the image of the God and Father of Jesus Christ. As a result, racism not only denies the unity of all humankind; it also refuses to acknowledge that being in the image of God means having "dominion over the earth." Human beings were created in the image and likeness of God. In the Bible, "image" and "likeness" do not allude to any kind of *physical* likeness, but rather describe our unique relationship to God. The likeness is not so much morphological as functional, dynamic.

The creation stories in Genesis 1 and 2 are an attempt to give expression to this creaturely relatedness to God. The responsibility that flows from this relationship is "dominion over creation." This has not only to do with the source of this power (God), but also with those with whom we are to share this unique gift: our fellow human beings. At the same time, we are reminded in Genesis 2 that this "dominion" is *service,* that there is an interdependence between human beings and an interdependence between human beings and physical creation. To have this dominion is to share this dominion. This is to be truly human. It means to be able *to be,* to live in accordance with one's God-given humanity. It means to be able to realize this essential humanity in the sociohistorical world in which we have responsibility.

To share in this dominion as a free person created by God enables human beings to become the subject of their humanity, to assume responsibility, to act responsibly, and in so acting to realize their own being and that of others. All this is denied by racism. It usurps the right to be truly human for itself alone and it tries to justify itself by relegating other groups to a subhuman level. Other groups are not truly human; or are not "equal"; or they are "equal, but. . . ."

Racism is a form of idolatry in which the dominant group assumes for itself a status higher than that of other groups in society. By its political, military, and economic power it seeks to play God in the lives of others. The history of white racism is replete with examples of it.

Racism has brought dehumanization, has undermined black personhood, destroyed the human-beingness of those who are called to be the children of God. It has caused those who are the image of the living God to despise themselves. They cannot understand why it should be their blackness that calls forth such hatred, such contempt, such wanton, terrible violence.

Most of all, racism denies the liberating, humanizing, reconciling work of Christ, the promised one who has taken on human form, thereby reaffirming human worth in the sight of God. Through his life he gave flesh and blood to the words of the psalmist concerning the weak and needy: "From oppression and violence he redeems their life; and precious is their blood in his sight" (Ps. 72:14).

Through his life, death, and resurrection Christ has reconciled human beings to God and to themselves; he has broken down the wall of partition and enmity, and so has become our peace (Eph. 2:14). He has brought us together in the one Lord, one faith, one baptism, one God who is the Father of us all (Eph. 4:5, 6).

Racism has not only contaminated human society; it has also defiled the very body of Christ. And it is Christians who have provided the moral and theological justification for racism and human degradation.

In 1981 South African society is still based on white racism and is maintained by escalating violence and oppression. Legalized discrimination is still a way of life. Apartheid means that, as recently as 1970, whites, only 17.8 percent of the population, received 71.9 percent of the national income; blacks received only 19.3 percent. It means that white greed and avarice claim 87 percent of the land; 13 percent is "allotted" to blacks. Apartheid means that blacks are denied any meaningful participation in the political decision-making process, so that the very word "democracy" has become a farce. It means a capitalistic economic structure for which atrocities such as the migrant labor system become a necessity. South African economist Dr. Francis Wilson has written in this regard:

> [This system] can, and does, compel old people living amongst their friends and relatives in familiar surroundings where they have spent their entire working lives to endure resettlement in some distant place where they feel they have been cast off to die. This system can, and does, force a man who wants to build a house with his wife and children to live instead for all his working life in "bachelor" barracks, so far away from his loved ones that he sees them only briefly once a year, and his children grow up without his influence, regarding him as a stranger. One may close one's mind to these facts; one may dismiss them as being isolated casualties for the sake of a greater goal; but the harsh reality is that there are hundreds of thousands of people in South Africa who are cruelly affected in this way.[3]

Apartheid means that the most important thing about a person is not that he or she is a human being created in the image of God with inalienable rights, but is his or her racial identity. It is racial identity that determines everything else in a person's life with an overwhelming intensity. Apartheid means that hundreds of children must die every year not only from hunger and malnutrition amid the South African plenty, but mercilessly shot down by riot police on the streets of our townships. But why go on? I do not want to give the impression that the terrible human suffering caused by this system can be described in words.

South Africa is not the only place in the world where oppression and exploitation are the daily bread of the poor and the defenseless. What is unique, however, is the role of the churches, more specifically, the Reformed churches. In a very important address given in 1980, the Rev. D. P. Botha showed conclusively that the present policy of apartheid is essentially the missionary policy of the white Dutch Reformed Church. The white Dutch Reformed Church has not only provided a theological justification for this policy; it also worked out, in considerable detail, the policy itself. It was the white Dutch Reformed Church that, from 1932 on, sent delegation after delegation to the government to support proposals for racial legislation. It worked hard to devise practical policies of apartheid that could be implemented by the government, while formulating theological constructs to justify the policy. It was these plans the church finally presented to the Nationalist Party in 1947. The Nationalist Party accepted them and the program won at the polls in 1948.[4]

It is no wonder that the *Kerkbode,* official mouthpiece of the white Dutch Reformed Church, wrote with pride in 1958: "As a church, we have always worked purposefully for the separation of the races. In this regard apartheid can rightfully be called a church policy."[5]

In fact, Botha says: "The role of organizations like the F.A.K and the *Broederbond* [outspoken pro-apartheid groups] fade into insignificance compared to the overwhelming role of the church [the white Dutch Reformed church] in preparing the Afrikaner to accept and vote for a socio-political program that will revolutionize South African life."[6]

And this policy is "all-embracing, soteriologically loaded," complete with a theology to rationalize it. As such it has become a pseudo-gospel, challenging the authority of the true gospel in the lives of all South Africans. The white Reformed churches in South Africa have not yet been able to repent, to correct their stand on the basis of a new understanding of the gospel. In spite of all the open human suffering, the violence necessary to maintain the system, and the damage done to the church of Jesus Christ, apartheid still has their support. Our Reformed churches have been divided on the basis of race and color, a situation that is still defended as a truthful expression of the will of God and a correct understanding of the church.

Within the Reformed family, racism has made it virtually impossible to share with one another that most significant act within the community of the faithful, a natural expression of the unity of the body of Christ: the Lord's Supper. And so both white and black Reformed Christians are deprived of the meaning of the sacrament that Calvin so much wanted to impress upon our minds:

> Now since he has only one body, of which he makes us all partakers, it is necessary that all of us also be made one body by such participation. . . . We shall benefit very much from the Sacrament if this thought is impressed and engraved upon our minds: that none of the brethren can be injured, despised, rejected, abused, or in any kind offended by us, without at the same time, injuring, despising, and abusing Christ by the wrongs we do; that we cannot disagree with our brethren without at the same time disagreeing with Christ; that we cannot love Christ without loving him in the brethren; that we ought to take the same care of our brethren's bodies as we take care of our own; for they are members of our body; and that, as no part of our body is touched by any feeling of pain which is not spread among all the rest, so we ought not to allow a brother to be affected by any evil, without being touched with compassion for him.[7]

Challenge to the World Alliance of Reformed Churches

The World Alliance of Reformed Churches is a confessional family. The rationale for its existence, the *strength* of its existence, is the uniqueness and significance of the Reformed tradition and its contribution to the witness of the church of Jesus Christ in the world. It is clear that the World Alliance of Reformed Churches has a special responsibility in this particular situation. Since 1976 the crisis in South Africa has taken on frightening proportions. The events of 1980 underscored it and the blood of hundreds of children is a chilling reminder of the sacrifices needed to still the cravings of the Moloch that apartheid has become. It is in the light of this that black Christians have said:

> We realize that the racial situation in this country has reached a critical stage and that God is calling the church as a liberating and reconciling community to identify itself with the oppressed and the poor in their struggle for the dignity which is theirs as human persons created in the image of the Triune God.[8]

The World Alliance of Reformed Churches has no less than ten member churches in South Africa. The vast majority of them form the "poor and oppressed" that the statement above refers to. They have a right to know what the Reformed tradition has to say about their situation. As far as the white member churches are concerned, they have the direct responsibility and the power to change the situation fundamentally, if they wish to. They should be addressed in terms of that responsibility and in terms of the historical development of apartheid as regards the churches. The World Alliance of Reformed Churches should accept the challenge to condemn apartheid as undergirded by the gospel and presented as commensurate with the Reformed tradition by the white Dutch Reformed churches in South Africa.

The World Alliance of Reformed Churches should reaffirm that racism is a sin, should reaffirm its support for the World

Council of Churches, and should encourage those member churches who are also members of the World Council of Churches to continue their prayerful support of the WCC Program to Combat Racism.

With regard to the South African situation, the World Alliance of Reformed Churches should accept its special responsibility. It should declare that apartheid, in the words of the 1978 synod of the Dutch Reformed Mission Church, is "irreconcilable with the gospel of Jesus Christ." If this is true, and if apartheid is also a denial of the Reformed tradition, then it should be declared a heresy.

To accept the Reformed confession is more than a formal acknowledgment of doctrine. Churches that accept the confession thereby commit themselves to show in their daily witness and service that the gospel has empowered them to live as the people of God. They also commit themselves to accept in their worship and at the table of the Lord the brothers and sisters who accept the same confession. Confessional subscription should lead to concrete manifestation in unity, in worship, and in working together at the common tasks of the church. It is one thing when the rules and laws of unjust and oppressive governments make this difficult or impossible for the church. But it is quite another thing when churches *willingly* and *purposefully* reject this unity and togetherness for reasons of racial prejudice, as the white Reformed churches of South Africa consistently have done.

In South Africa, as I have noted, apartheid is not just a political ideology. Its very existence as a political policy has depended and still depends on the theological justification by certain member churches of the World Alliance of Reformed Churches. For Reformed churches, this situation should constitute a *status confessionis*: Reformed churches should recognize that apartheid is heresy, contrary to the gospel and inconsistent with the Reformed tradition. Consequently the Reformed churches should reject apartheid as such.

I realize that this may be a difficult issue for the World Alliance of Reformed Churches. But it is an issue too long deferred. It would be well to remember the words of Dietrich Bonhoeffer, that fearless partisan in the service of Jesus Christ, as he spoke to the ecumenical movement at a time not unlike that in South Africa today:

> Not to act and not to take a stand, simply for fear of making a mistake, when others have to make infinitely difficult decisions every day, seems to me to be almost a contradiction of love. . . . Too late means "never." If the ecumenical movement does not see this now and if there are none who are "violent to take heaven by force" (Matt. 11:12), then the ecumenical movement is no longer the church, but a useless association for making fine speeches.[9]

And, in terms of the meaning of racism, remember the words of Calvin as he comments on 1 Corinthians 7:23: "That we have been redeemed by Christ at so great a price as our redemption cost him, so that we should not enslave ourselves to the wicked desires of men—much less be subject to their impiety."[10]

Chapter XI

The Present Crisis in Apartheid: A Reply to the South African Government Proposal for a Three-Tier Parliament

We are meeting at a time of crisis. Apartheid is in a crisis. This grandiloquent ideal, brought into the world and held before the eyes of white South Africa as an all-encompassing, soteriologically loaded policy of racial separation, which would solve all the problems of this country, is beginning to disintegrate. The pseudo-religious nature of the ideology of apartheid has been unmasked unmercifully. Churches in South Africa and elsewhere have branded apartheid a heresy and have stated quite unequivocally that any church that defends this policy cannot be regarded as an authentic member of the body of Christ.

Internally, the courageous resistance to apartheid and the determination of black South Africans to be free have made it clear to white South Africans in no uncertain terms that there can be no peaceful existence for them in this land unless it is peaceful coexistence with blacks. Little by little, the international community has come to understand the danger that the policy of apartheid poses to the stability of the region and to international peace. The

This address was given at the conference of the Anti–South African Indian Council Committee held in Johannesburg, Jan. 23, 1983.

total rejection by blacks of the policies of the present government has put the lie to its claim that apartheid is the solution to our problems. The shame of racism, the brutal violence needed to sustain the system, the naked greed it tries to conceal, the stunning hypocrisy it generates, the sheer dishonesty in its assertions of the changes that are said to take place—all this now stands exposed for all who have eyes to see.

The New Constitutional Proposals

The South African government is tackling the present crisis by changes in the Constitution and the political system. The government and its supporters insist that apartheid has failed only partly—namely, in not providing political space for the so-called coloureds and Indians. Apartheid is succeeding, however, they assert, in that the homelands policy makes provision for the political and human needs of the almost 25 million black South Africans.

Blacks are not impressed. We have seen what has happened in the homelands. We know that the "independence" of the four Bush Republics is a sham; that the homelands are no more than dumping grounds for the discarded blacks of this land; that they are places where our elderly die of misery and want, and our children are stalked day and night by hunger, sickness, and the grim death that sits on the shoulder of hopelessness. These homelands are places where the signs and tokens of apartheid have been replaced by the relentless grip of black dictatorship. The government and its supporters know that these impoverished patches of land will never attain economic independence; that there will always be more blacks in so-called white South Africa than in the homelands; that the very way in which the homelands were set up is the greatest stumbling block to democratic rule there; that this policy is beyond description in its immorality. But they are undeterred. For them, to quote a delegate of the white Dutch Reformed Church to the World Alliance of Reformed Churches meeting in Ottawa, "the homelands policy is the ultimate solution to the problems of South Africa."

At present, a vexing problem involved in apartheid policy has to do with persons classified as coloureds and Indians. A solution to *this* problem has produced the new constitutional proposals. The so-called coloureds and Indians may join with whites in a three-chamber parliament, divided on an ethnic basis, with whites in the majority. The whites will remain firmly in control. Greater economic benefits constitute the incentive for coloured and Indian cooperation in the new structure. Coloured and Indian officials will gain a degree of control over separate coloured and Indian affairs and will participate in joint consultation on common affairs.

We blacks are being told that we have our "political rights" in the homelands; it is "unjust" for coloureds and Indians not to have the "same rights." Suddenly the government's problems with the coloureds and Indians have become *our* problems! The crisis of apartheid has become *our* crisis!

We blacks are being told that the decisions we make in "our homelands" will determine not only our own immediate future, but also the future of our children. These decisions will determine the nature of the struggle for freedom and human dignity that will surely continue. Coloureds and Asians should likewise have a voice in determining *their* future. Has any national government ever been more conspicuously hypocritical? Suddenly there are no more "lepers" in South Africa!

We must remind ourselves of some facts. Those who are talking this way are the ones who came to power in 1948 on a blatantly racist platform. They are the ones who took British segregationist policies and made them into a system that is terrifying in its totality and effectiveness. They are the ones who spent years trying to get the last few blacks off the voters' role, and finally succeeded by packing the Senate and twisting justice in the courts. They are the ones who passed law after law to entrench racism: laws on racial classifications, group areas, mixed marriages, separate education, the homeland policy. All these laws stripped Africans of South African citizenship. These are the ones who wanted the land, and took it; they saw our homes and claimed them. They built their palaces and their economic kingdom on the blood, sweat, and tears of our people. When we blacks resisted, we were hounded, jailed, exiled, detained without trial, tortured, and killed. Our peaceful demonstrations were turned into massacres: Sharpeville, Soweto, Cape Town. *All this they want us simply to forget.*

When white South Africans thought that they had broken our spirit, they gave us dummy institutions; they humiliated us with puppet leaders whom they themselves never would have accepted were they to have been in our place. This effort failed because of the refusal of the vast majority of the population to accept anything less than full democratic rights.

Now we are faced with this new situation. The steadfast determination of blacks to fight for their human dignity, their successful recourse to the politics of refusal, the growing realization in the world (in spite of the Reagan administration in the USA!) that apartheid is a cancer in the body politic of the world, and the subsequent pressures on South Africa—through all this it has finally dawned on the government that something must be done.

The government says that the Westminster parliamentary system cannot work in South Africa. That is its basic point of departure. In our turn we ask: Why will it not work? There was nothing wrong with the Westminster system when it gave the Nationalists a winner-takes-all majority in the white parliament. There was nothing wrong with the Westminster system when it gave white South Africans the right to make laws for the whole of this nation, even though its officials were elected by a small white minority. There was nothing wrong with the Westminster system when it gave white South Africans an excuse to use the word "democracy," although they knew they were oppressing blacks and excluding us from meaningful political participation. Now that the pressures for change are becoming hard to resist, now that real majority rule is staring them in the face, *now* they discover that the Westminster system will not work.

Perhaps white South Africans say the Westminster system will not work because the Nationalists themselves have set such a bad example within this system. They use Westminster-style democracy as a cover for totalitarian rule. They use Parliament to enact laws that would have been labeled criminal if there had been an independent judiciary. They use the system to cover up shameful acts of dishonesty, as we saw in "the information scandal." Now they are afraid that blacks will do the same to them if the system remains. Because, moreover, they are religious persons, the white South Africans know that what the Bible says in this regard is true: "You shall reap what you sow."

The system they are now proposing harbors within its bosom the same danger. If one day blacks take over the government and a black electoral college elects a black executive president with such sweeping, almost dictatorial, powers and he sends the white Parliament home because it does not agree with him—what then? Shall we hear the same crocodile lament that we are hearing about Zimbabwe where the new government uses Mr. Ian Smith's laws to keep him in check and now Mr. Smith is angry?

There must be no doubt whatsoever in our minds. These proposals cannot be accepted and there can be no cooperation with the government on this basis. We must reject the government-proposed constitutional changes for clear reasons:

1) It is clear that these proposals are an entrenchment of apartheid and white domination.

2) The proposals accept as a basic premise that "the homeland policy of the South African government is irreversible."

3) The basic tenets of apartheid—the laws that are the lifeblood of the system—remain intact: racial classification, group areas, separate education, the so-called security laws, and the like.

4) Within the system as proposed there will not really be opportunity to change these laws: they fall under the jurisdiction of the white Parliament; and the new system is designed specifically to prevent coalitions with other groups, walkouts, and boycotts.

5) Despite attempts to create the illusion of an "independent" President's Council with an "independent" contribution, it is quite clear that these proposals were devised to give shape to P. W. Botha's brand of Nationalist policy, geared to the needs of a streamlined apartheid. We had no part whatsoever in their making and in their interpretation. These proposals were designed to appease the Nationalist Party Congresses that debated and accepted them. Quite apart from the fact that we are sick and tired of being "done for" and spoken down to, there is no reason in the world why we should place our future in the hands of those who

for so many decades now have shown with unabashed clarity that they do not have our interests at heart.

6) The proposals quite unashamedly accept ethnicity as the indispensable basis for doing politics in South Africa. All democratic minded persons in South Africa have rejected this premise because we know that ethnicity does not solve differences; it, rather, entrenches them. Ethnicity tends to emphasize group interests, keeps alive tendencies toward tribalism, white and black, and fosters narrow, ethnic nationalism that can only aggravate an already volatile situation. Furthermore, ethnicity is inseparable from racism, however subtle it may be. The insidious nature of this evil is a warning that societies such as ours have enough problems without exacerbating their inherent racism by making ethnicity a basic, politically divisive factor.

7) These proposals exclude the majority of the South African nation, and, as such, they constitute a recipe for violent confrontation and disaster.

8) These proposals are not only politically untenable; they are also morally wrong and unacceptable. As a Christian I cannot and will not accept responsibility for the continuation of apartheid, a system that, in the words of Bishop Desmond Tutu, is the greatest evil since Nazism.

It is morally wrong to accept for myself rights and privileges when such rights and privileges are denied others who are fellow South Africans. We must say once more: justice denied to one is justice denied to all. With these proposals the injustices of apartheid will not be removed, and justice will continue to lie prostrate on the streets of our cities. Peace will find no refuge in this land until all of God's children in South Africa have the simple and indispensable dignity of full human rights.

In 1977, when the government first made new constitutional proposals, the Labour Party rejected them for the following reasons: (1) They entrenched apartheid. (2) They were devised exclusively by the government; the South African people had no part in their formulation. (3) They would mean the inclusion of coloureds and Indians, and the exclusion of blacks. (4) They entrenched white domination.

What is the difference between the proposals of 1977 and the new proposals of the President's Council? There are no essential differences. Yet the Labour Party and the South African Indian Council have accepted the new proposals. It is clear that once again the voice of Mammon has spoken louder than the voice of principle.

The new partners of the government are being validated constitutionally. These are the junior partners in apartheid. From now on they will share the responsibility for apartheid, for the creation of yet more homelands, for the resettlement of more blacks, for the ongoing rape of our human dignity, for the death of those who resist this evil system. They will be co-responsible for the continuation—yes, the enhancement—of the civil war in which South Africa is already engaged. From now on, in terms of active planning and legislation, apartheid no longer has only a white face.

There is a great sadness in all of this and a persistent measure of inevitability. One ought not to play around with evil. Working within the system, for whatever reason, contaminates you. It wears down your defenses, it makes easier the rationalizations needed for staying in the system. It makes you susceptible to the hidden and not so hidden persuasions that are at work within every system. It whets your appetite for power. The system even allows you some petty victories, so that you believe you can actually beat it. All the while it draws you closer, blunting your judgment, and finally exposes your powerlessness as you "join the system to fight the system." What you call "compromise" for the sake of politics is in fact selling out your principles, your ideals, and the future of your children.

This situation calls for vigilance. We must not compromise the struggle we have been engaged in for well nigh a century. We may not betray the ideals we have, the belief in a truly democratic South Africa. We must not betray the blood of our children. Today we are saying to South Africa: we will not do it! The dream of justice, of a free nation, of a humanized society, has not died. Those who have made compromises never understood this dream, have never been part of this struggle.

Our response to the crisis facing us today is a dialectical one. It is the politics of refusal, which has within it both a yes and a no.

We must continue to struggle for the liberation, freedom, and human dignity of all persons in South Africa. While we say yes to *this* struggle, we say no to apartheid, racial segregation, and the economic exploitation of the oppressed masses in South Africa.

We must continue to show South Africa and the world that there are blacks who refuse to be intimidated by the violence of apartheid or be tempted by the sugar-coated fruits of apartheid. While we say no, therefore, to hollow solutions built on personal gain and petty group self-interest, we say yes to integrity and commitment.

We must continue to work for a safe and secure future for our children, for a society where they will not be infected by the poison of racism. While we say yes, therefore, to a future built on genuine peace and justice, we say no to building that future on participation in greed, exploitation, and the narrow nationalisms that carry within themselves the seeds of destruction. We must refuse to let our children die in a war that is being waged for the protection of apartheid and the South African neocolonialist designs on Namibia and for frustrating the hopes of the Namibian people for freedom, democracy, and genuine independence.

This is the politics of refusal, and it is the only dignified response that blacks can give in this situation. In order to succeed we need a united front. Most of the Christian churches, and all of the democratically minded organizations in our communities, have rejected unequivocally the proposals of the President's Council and the call to cooperate in their implementation. We all are committed to the struggle for a nonracist, open, democratic South Africa, a unitary state, one nation in which all citizens will have the rights accorded them by ordinance of almighty God. There is no reason why churches, civic associations, trade unions, student organizations, and sports bodies should not unite on this issue, pool our resources, inform the people of the fraud that is about to be perpetrated in its name, and on the day of the election expose these plans for what they are.

Two Versions of Basically the Same Policy

Those who have opted to join the government have agreed that it is necessary in order to "help Mr. P. W. Botha against Dr.

Treurnicht'' or to help Mr. Botha in his fight against the ''right wing'' in his own party, because Mr. Botha is on ''the right road.'' This argument is as incongruous as it is incomprehensible. Apart from the fact that nobody, including the Nationalist Party leadership, is certain precisely what Mr. Botha's road leads to, what business do blacks have trying to alleviate the problems caused by tensions within the Nationalist Party or within Afrikanerdom? To be sure, the turmoil within Afrikanerdom and the split in the Nationalist Party have been the most hopeful signs in white politics for many years. This is in fact exactly what we need. More turmoil means more creative tension, undermining the self-confidence and the arrogance that have become the hallmark of those in power for far too long. It means opening up possibilities for a realignment in white politics, for detribalization, and for more effective opposition.

Why would any black person wish to stop this process? It would be a blessing if this government were to fall. This would help to bring about the real, fundamental changes this government is so effectively obstructing. Moreover, do not the ''joiners'' know that there is no fundamental difference between Mr. Botha and Dr. Treurnicht? The argument between these two gentlemen is not about the ideology of apartheid; it is not about whether apartheid ought to be removed or not. It is not about whether South Africa is to become an open, democratic society, or whether Africans should retain their citizenship in this country. They are not arguing about the necessity of white domination; they are not in disagreement on the issue of white control over the economy. The dispute is not about removing the racist laws from the statute books or about universal franchise. It is not about ways to redistribute the wealth of the country.

The real issue, the only issue, between Mr. Botha and Dr. Treurnicht is the most effective way in which white control of the economy and white political domination can survive in South Africa at this particular point in history in which pressure is being brought to bear on the government. In other words, the argument is about how to do the same thing in order to have all things remain the same.

Dr. Treurnicht believes that white domination in politics as well as in the economy can be maintained by unchanged and unabashed racial separation, overt oppression, and a romantic call to the beleaguered Afrikaners to risk isolation as they cling tenaciously to their beliefs and depend only on their history, the conviction of their righteousness, their gun and their God.

Mr. Botha, on the other hand, having a better understanding of the world today, believes there is an alternative solution to the present crisis in South Africa. His solution is to streamline apartheid (permits, mixed sports, etc.,) to allow limited participation by coloureds and Asians in politics and the economy under strict white control (which he calls power-sharing), and to generate the illusion of a challenge to the old, Afrikaner romanticism. By doing this, Mr. Botha has succeeded in four ways. He has (1) created distance between himself and Dr. Treurnicht, though it is mostly imaginary; (2) caused confusion in the ranks of English-speakers who now feel that Mr. Botha is indeed moving somewhere and who cannot understand why their opposition party is so "negative" ("After all, coloureds are playing for Western Province, and soon they will be in Parliament. What more do they want?"); (3) lured some coloureds and Indians into this trap with the hope that more middle-class coloureds and Indians will join up; and (4) created the illusion of change so that conservative, Western governments can support his government openly "with good reason."

What really matters, as I have shown, has not changed at all. The government has created a warm, cozy, middle ground where everyone who comes in may have their ethnic piece of the pie as long as no fundamental questions are asked. Many, including even some of the media, are coming in, hoping somewhere there will be a reward for them, and that, miraculously, the agony caused by apartheid will end. Those who refuse to do so are branded "leftists," "radicals," and "politically naive." But that does not matter; this situation is only temporary: *truth crushed to earth shall rise again,* and *no lie can live forever.*

I want to remind those Western governments that are now satisfied with this government that they should not be misled. The blacks of this country *know* what they want, and it is not this. They know who their leaders are, and they are not sell-outs who need the Nationalist press to protect them against the wrath of their own people. We shall not be satisfied until we have our full human rights. Why can Britain go to war, in the words of Mrs. Thatcher, "so that the people of the Falklands may have the right to live freely under the government of their choice," but we are denied that right? Why can Americans have a system guaranteeing the equality of all under the law and justice for all, but we are denied it? The test of a good South African government will not be made in Washington, or London, or Moscow; it will be made right here in this land. That test will be made by the suffering, struggling oppressed whose determination to be free shall not be undermined by the violence of Pretoria or by the thinly veiled cynicism of Washington.

I want to conclude by reminding you of three little words that express eloquently our seriousness in this struggle. The first word is *all.* We want *all* our rights; not just some, not just those that the government sees fit to give. We want all of them. We want *all* South Africans to have their rights; not just a select few, not just coloureds and Indians after they are made honorary whites. We want rights for *all* South Africans, including those whose citizenship has already been stripped away by this government.

The second word is *here.* We want all our rights right *here*—in South Africa, in a united South Africa. We do not want them in impoverished homelands; we do not want them in our separate little group areas. We want them here, in this land, which one day we shall once again call our own.

The third word is *now.* We want our rights *now.* We have been waiting so long; we have been struggling so long. We have pleaded, petitioned, cried, marched, been jailed, exiled, killed for too long. *Now* is the time.

As we struggle let us remember that change does not roll in on the wheels of inevitability. It comes, rather, through the tireless efforts of men and women who are willing to be co-workers with God (Martin Luther King, Jr., for example). Let us continue to believe that freedom will come; that justice will one day no longer stumble in the streets; that violence will cease and peace will reign; that racism and apartheid will be merely a bad dream neither remembered nor mourned; that hatred will make place for love and true humanity. Let us believe the words of the prophet and work for the day when:

> Babies will no longer die in infancy, and all people will live out their life span. People will build houses and they will live in them—they will not be used by someone else. They will plant vineyards and enjoy the wine—it will not be drunk by others. The work they do will be successful, and their children will not meet with disaster [Isa. 65:20–23].

Chapter XII

Apartheid after the WARC Decisions in Ottawa, 1982

It is good for me, as a member of WARC (World Alliance of Reformed Churches), to become acquainted with you, the Remonstrant Brotherhood, in this way, and to be able to tell you explicitly that my goal as president is that together we may make this organization into something filled with life and power and hope. If we are not able to do this, I do not know what my role should be during my tenure as president of WARC.

In August 1982, WARC, during its meeting in Ottawa, Canada, made some fundamental, radical decisions relative to South Africa. WARC made several other very important decisions during that meeting, but from the beginning of that meeting the South African question was paramount. And with good reason. In a public declaration, WARC condemned apartheid as sinful, rejected it, and declared theological justification of apartheid to be theological heresy, error, and a repudiation of the gospel. WARC also accepted the *status confessionis* classification of apartheid. By this we meant that apartheid is not merely a political matter. Apartheid, rather, threatens faith in Jesus Christ, threatens the integrity of the gospel, and threatens the credibility

This address was delivered by Dr. Boesak in his role as president of the World Alliance of Reformed Churches to the general assembly of the Remonstrant Brotherhood Executive Committee in Hoogeveen, the Netherlands, on June 4, 1983.

of the church of Jesus Christ. WARC took the position that apartheid endangers our confession "Jesus is the Lord." We reasoned that no one can say that Jesus is the Lord *and* maintain that apartheid can be called Christian, as is done in South Africa. We said that these two positions are mutually exclusive.

In addition, we suspended the privileges of membership in WARC of two white South African churches: the Nederduits Hervormde Kerk van Afrika and the Nederduits Gereformeerde Kerk van Zuid Afrika. These churches were given a type of observer status until it becomes evident that they meet the following conditions: they are not closed to blacks; blacks and whites can celebrate the eucharist together in these churches; these churches take a strong position against apartheid; these white churches identify themselves with the victims of apartheid, with the struggle for the extension of justice and humanity to all South Africans; and these churches in cooperation with the other South African churches seek reconciliation and justice, as well as the dismantling of apartheid in church and state. If this takes place, if there are signs that this is taking place, then we shall welcome these churches to full fellowship in WARC once more.

You may ask, of course, if these conditions are not too difficult. Ought we not to relate to one another in the Christian church in a way different from what these conditions stipulate? Does not this decision attempt too much too quickly? Must we not be more tolerant of one another? Have we not had enough misery in the Christian community as a result of churches quickly jumping on one another's backs? Have we not far too often been too narrow-minded in our thoughts about and dealings with one another in the Christian community? Should we not be more broad-minded with one another? These are legitimate questions.

A Long History

I wish to state emphatically, dear brothers and sisters, that I believe the WARC decision to be the only one that we could have made with honesty and integrity. And I shall indicate why this is true. There are, above all, two reasons for the necessity of the WARC decision. The first reason is that this decision represents the climax of a long historical process during which the "ecumenical movement" attempted to persuade the white Reformed churches in South Africa to reject apartheid because it is an unchristian policy. The Ottawa meeting in 1982 was not the first time that WARC involved itself in the question of racism and apartheid. The churches throughout the world and the ecumenical movement have involved themselves with the question of racism for more than sixty years. The International Missionary Council addressed itself to the problems of colonialism and racism in the Jerusalem conference in 1928.

As early as 1928, the churches were confronted with the following questions: What connection is there between racism and the colonization of large areas of the world? How is it that the Western churches can live comfortably with racism and colonialism? Why do racism and colonialism not trouble the Western churches? Why do the Western churches not question the meaning of racism and colonialism in terms of their victims, and also in terms of the role of the church as church in the world? It can be said that the Jerusalem meeting of the International Missionary Council did not contribute substantially to a resolution of the problems of racism and colonialism. It is important, however, to establish the historical fact that the Jerusalem 1928 conference, in an honest and forthright manner, put these questions on the agenda of the ecumenical movement.

At the subsequent meeting of the International Missionary Council at Tambaram, Madras, India, in 1938, and at meetings during the 1930s and '40s of Life and Work, one of the movements that led to the formation of the World Council of Churches, questions pertaining to racism and colonialism were discussed. These questions, however, were not the central issues of those assemblies. At the time, it was merely judged to be "beneficial" to discuss these questions. It is always difficult to address significantly and urgently an issue that is peripheral to what, at the moment, is regarded as the central issue. It is difficult to have a significant, open discussion of an issue that, at the moment, need not be dealt with day after day after day. Consequently, in the 1930s and '40s, although racism and colonialism were discussed in the ecumenical movement, they were not pressing, urgent issues in the churches—that is, the "older" churches, the Western churches.

The situation changed in 1948. In 1948 the World Council of Churches (WCC) was organized and assembled in Amsterdam for its first general assembly. Amsterdam was a place where participants were able to see all about them the clearly visible signs of the Second World War, which Europe will never forget. And Europe will never forget that that war was started by Germany, and that, at the heart of that war, there was a racist ideology. Then for the first time Europe experienced at first hand what happens when racism has a significant say in the life and thought of a people in a particular area of the world. At that time we all saw what was happening and we all knew that things were not going well with the Jews in Germany and elsewhere. At that time the churches could not evade the issue of racism. There was no longer any excuse. The Christian churches were forced to confess that racism was the heart of the matter in the holocaust. We were forced to confess that we could make no judgment about racism other than this: it is an unholy, demonic ideology. We made that confession. We did it.

At the same time, however, in 1948, the Nationalist Party was chosen to organize and lead the government in South Africa. Then, for the first time, the term apartheid appeared on the horizon of world politics. But the churches in Europe were not very sensitive to what was happening in South Africa. They knew that something was happening, but they did not know how important it was. This the European churches knew only later, when one racial law after another was enacted in South Africa. The European churches understood the importance of what had begun in 1948 in South Africa when they saw with increasing clarity the oppression to which the black population was being subjected. The European churches understood the importance of what began in 1948 when they saw the unholy alliance that developed between the Afrikaner churches and the Afrikaner government.

When the WCC met in Evanston in 1954, the assembly discussed racism. But it did not wish to have a confrontation on this issue. The assembly reasoned that we human beings must all live together. We must attempt to resolve this issue as Christians. We do not wish to alienate one another. Above all, we do not wish to alienate the white churches of South Africa. We want the white churches of South Africa to join us in our common work. Therefore, a pastoral letter was addressed to the white churches of South Africa, a letter in which the WCC upheld the position that apartheid is a clear manifestation of oppression—a position that the white churches of South Africa should recognize also. The pastoral letter went on to say that the reconciliation which the WCC seeks to effect among the Christian peoples in South Africa is possible through the power of the gospel and through the Spirit of our Lord. The Nederduits Gereformeerde Kerk van Zuid Afrika, at that time a member of the WCC, never discussed this pastoral letter in its assemblies.

Then the Sharpville massacre took place. During a peaceful demonstration by blacks against apartheid, more than eighty persons were killed and more than a hundred were wounded. Most of the victims were shot in the back. This event shocked the churches in South Africa. Sharpville, in fact, shocked the entire world. Then questions were raised: How could Sharpville happen? Why were we unable to prevent it? What must we, as churches, do? Does the church share the guilt involved in Sharpville?

Through the intervention of the WCC, the Cottesloe Consultation took place in Johannesburg, South Africa, in 1961, and these questions were posed. Later the Nederduits Gereformeerde Kerk and the Nederduits Hervormde Kerk dissociated themselves from their own representatives in the Cottesloe Consultation. Both churches repudiated the report of the consultation. Dr. H. F. Verwoerd, who was the prime minister in South Africa at the time, said publicly that he did not accept the report of the Cottesloe Consultation, because he knew that the official position of the churches was supportive of apartheid. Therefore, he concluded, he would wait to see what judgment the synods of the white churches would make as their response to the Cottesloe Consultation. What did the synods do? One after the other, they said, "No, we will have nothing to do with the report. We dissociate ourselves from the delegates." The only delegate who remained steadfast at that time was the Rev. C. F. Beyers Naudé.

Then came the New Delhi General Assembly of the WCC in 1961. At this assembly the International Missionary Council and the WCC united to form one organization. The Nederduits Gereformeerde Kerk withdrew from the WCC. In 1968 the WCC met in Uppsala. This assembly made the decision to inaugurate the Program to Combat Racism.

What position has WARC taken up relative to racism? WARC met in Frankfurt in 1964 and stated emphatically that racism cannot be regarded as Christian. Racism must be rejected as an idolatry. Once again representatives of South African churches were asked and urged to discuss this matter with one another when they returned to South Africa. The white churches, as the stronger churches, the ones that should take the initiative, were asked to inaugurate a conversation among the churches in South Africa. This urgent request was ignored.

In 1970 WARC assembled in Nairobi, Kenya. It concluded that a church that makes racism or racial segregation a norm for itself cannot be regarded as an authentic member of the body of Jesus Christ. This is strong language! Once again the white churches of South Africa were asked to address the matter of racism in concert with the black churches. Once more this request was ignored.

Hence, when we arrived in Ottawa in 1982, the matter of racism was certainly not a new issue. It is not consistent with the facts to say that the decision that WARC made in Ottawa was precipitate. It is also not consistent with the facts to say that WARC has been impatient vis-à-vis the white churches of South Africa. This, rather, was the culmination of a process that had gone on for sixty years—a process in which the ecumenical movement attempted to talk with the churches in South Africa, and to point to history, very recent history, and say, "Please pay attention to this matter! It can result in a bloodbath in your country!"

This brief and sketchy historical survey suffices to highlight the appropriateness of the decision that WARC took with regard to the Nederduits Gereformeerde Kerk van Zuid Afrika and the Nederduits Hervormde Kerk van Afrika: the decision to suspend the membership of the two churches until the stated conditions are met.

Apartheid Intensified

There is a second reason why the WARC decision was appropriate and the only decision that WARC could make if it were to maintain its credibility and integrity: the harsh and cruel extension of apartheid to every area of society in South Africa. When we blacks were traveling to Ottawa we said to one another that things could not go on like this any longer. WARC has become a very important organization for us. Many of the black churches in South Africa are not members of the WCC. WARC is the only real ecumenical experience for those of us whose churches are not affiliated with the WCC. WARC is also the one great ecumenical organization with which the two white Dutch Reformed churches in South Africa still were affiliated in 1982.

Apartheid is not merely a word for us; it is a harsh and bitter reality. We have seen the South African government follow through ruthlessly with the homelands policy for the African population of South Africa. We have seen large numbers of Africans driven violently from their villages to resettlement camps, to live there in the most miserable of circumstances and, within a few years, to die there. In the richest land on the African continent and one of the richest lands in the world, today we still see black infants die of malnutrition before their first birthday, victims of kwashiorkor, or because they are not provided with medical care. We have seen millions of black South Africans deprived of their citizenship because the government has declared the arbitrarily defined homelands to be independent states. Suddenly one morning a person awakes with a shock: "I am no longer a South African."

We have seen the bitterness that apartheid unleashes not only in the hearts of the young, but also in the hearts of all those who still possess some self-respect. We have seen hundreds of thousands of persons legally robbed of a small piece of property that had been in their family for generations. It is done by reclassification of their land through application of the Group Areas Law. We have seen them, then, cast out on the plain in the Cape area or somewhere else in South Africa that has been designated as an area for "coloureds" or for "Indians" or for "blacks."

We have seen how squatters are dealt with in Capetown. We have seen what happens in the camp in Nyanga where women come from the homelands with their children to live together with their husbands. They say, "We wish to live together as a family." They come to the camp in Nyanga for this reason alone; for no other reason. This, however, they may not do, because, according to South African law, they may not live together as a family in Nyanga. Their family life is disrupted by the South African government. A man who brings his wife to Capetown so that they can live together as a family breaks the law: he illegally "gives accommodation" to a black. For doing this, the black husband can be imprisoned for six months. At this moment men and women are imprisoned in Capetown because as husbands and wives they wished to continue to live as families with their children. That, however, they may not do.

We have seen the wretchedly poor and inadequate huts these squatters have made out of pieces of planks, cardboard, and plastic so that they and their family can crawl in to seek protection from the cold Cape winter and from the rain. We have seen the police day after day raid these miserable huts at three o'clock in the morning to raze them and haul their occupants away to prison. If they resist, the police have used tear gas to subdue them. What mother would not resist the attempt to throw her child into prison?

In their attempt to enforce the Group Areas Law, the police have used dogs and guns also. In May 1983, after the police destroyed a squatters' camp, those who escaped attempted to shield themselves from the wind and the rain by spreading plastic over two or three bushes. They could crawl into this small space to seek refuge. The police, however, pulled the bushes out of the ground. One older woman, certainly more than sixty-five years of age, attempted to shield herself from the wind and rain by holding a piece of plastic over her head. A policeman came and cruelly took the piece of plastic from her. When one of the leaders of the camp asked the police if they thought the inhabitants were dogs who deserved treatment of this type, he was arrested and carted away to prison.

This sort of thing is happening *now* in South Africa. It is happening at this moment, when I am able to speak peacefully with you here in this place. This, however, is what apartheid is. And we have seen too much of it.

In 1976 the police shot and killed defenseless children on the streets in Soweto. In 1977 nineteen organizations, including the

Christian Institute, with which the Rev. Beyers Naudé was associated, were declared to be illegal organizations. In 1977 we also experienced the martyrdom in prison of Steve Biko. In 1980 we experienced the demonstrations of the schoolchildren in Capetown. There, also, we saw the police shoot and kill children on the street. I remember very well that at that time I was a member of a delegation that was to meet and speak with officers of the white Nederduits Gereformeerde Kerk of the Western Cape. The purpose of our meeting was to make a request of the white church: "You have influence with your government. It is, after all, your government. Will you ask the government to refrain from killing children?" That was all we asked. The officers of the church refused our request. The police could continue without interference. This happened, remember, in 1980.

When we arrived in Ottawa in 1982 for the WARC meeting, we thought that no one could or would plead for patience concerning something that has no right to exist: apartheid. In the circumstances, we thought that a Christian church certainly could not justify apartheid. This, however, did and does happen. We have experienced it. Apartheid, as you know, is not merely a political philosophy, but also a pseudo-religious ideology whose proponents, with their hand on the Bible, assert that apartheid is the only Christian, final solution to the South African problem. Someone said this in Ottawa also; Dr. Rossouw used these words. We all, moreover, have heard before the words "final solution."

In South Africa, therefore, dear brothers and sisters, we are not concerned in the first place with the life of blacks, important as that may be. We are not concerned, in the first place, with the future relationships of blacks and whites in South Africa, important as this may be. In South Africa we are concerned, primarily, with apartheid, and therefore with the word of God, with the gospel of Jesus Christ, with the integrity of the church of the Lord's witness.

If apartheid is Christian, then we can say, "Take your Christianity and go to hell." We, however, must assert very clearly and emphatically that the God of the Bible is not the God portrayed by the adherents of apartheid; and the gospel is not what is portrayed by the adherents of apartheid. You may not make the gospel equivalent to the death that is apartheid. And you may not make the injustice that apartheid constitutes equivalent to the God of justice and the Father of our Lord Jesus Christ. You certainly cannot do that. And if you cannot do that, we must say so in the strongest terms possible. This was the context in which I stated earlier that WARC had no other option in Ottawa in 1982. WARC could say only, "This is heresy. This is a repudiation of the heart of the gospel!"

By making this statement have we chased the white church away? No, rather, this is what we have said: "Continue to participate in the community of WARC. We do not wish to release you. We wish to hold on to you. We must, nevertheless, tell you unambiguously that the church has reached a point where it is necessary to state in unison, 'apartheid must come to an end!' "

You remember, undoubtedly, that, during the time of the Confessing Church in Germany, Dietrich Bonhoeffer tried for years to persuade the ecumenical movement not only to affirm the position of the Confessing Church, but also to repudiate the position of the "official" church in Germany. Bonhoeffer knew then, already, what we have since learned in South Africa: the one must be stated and put into effect along with the other. To affirm the Confessing Church in Germany was to repudiate the heresy that Hitler and Marxism belong within the Christian church. Dietrich Bonhoeffer did not succeed. I frequently wonder if the Confessing Church in Germany would still be exercising an influence, would still exist, if the ecumenical movement had recognized the importance of Bonhoeffer's plea.

As representatives of black South African churches, we did not go to Ottawa in 1982 with political intentions. We went, rather, with our hearts in our hands and we said, "We wish to hear a word from the churches relative to what is being done in South Africa: not a word in the name of Marx or Lenin or Stalin or Mao; but, rather, a word in the name of the Lord Jesus Christ and in the name of his church." Such a word would have enormous consequences for all of us. In South Africa we have discovered, to our surprise, that once you have said apartheid is heresy, no further words are necessary. Then you may not continue to talk as if apartheid could still be discussed on a theoretical or academic level.

In this context the focus is no longer on words, but rather on works. In this context the situation in South Africa makes demands on us because combating apartheid is an evangelical necessity. At present, the only way the black churches can respond to the command to live in obedience to the Lord is by opposing the government of South Africa. We have discovered we must say to our fellow church members, and not merely to the government, that whenever the government makes a law that conflicts with the word of the Lord and requires of us conduct that conflicts with what we know to be Christian and human, we are obligated to confess, "We must obey God rather than humans." To make this confession in South Africa demands readiness to be imprisoned. We, however, are only human. We are frightened, for we know that if one enters prison in South Africa, one has no guarantee of ever being released.

The churches are frightened, also; however, they too must speak out and embody the confession of the Christian faith. The church must make this confession relative to the mixed-marriages law. If a man and woman come to us and say they wish to marry in spite of the legal prohibition of their marriage because they are from different races, then we in the church must say, "We will marry you." We will take the risk. If it is true that love comes to persons from God, and if it is true that we receive one another as husband and wife from the hand of God, then we, as church, must make this confession to the government: "As a government, you have no right to separate this couple by means of a law." And then we must marry the couple. Doing so may mean that a pastor will lose his license to perform marriages. It may also mean that the pastor will be imprisoned for six months. But we as church shall be saying to the government explicitly and unambiguously, "In spite of the economic, political, and military power that you wield, we must let you see that you are not God!" This is what Desmond Tutu said to the minister of law and order, Louis Le Grange. "Mr. Minister, you are only a man. You are not a god. You ought not to attempt to conduct yourself like God. Your name shall remain in history books as an undefined scribble. The name of the Lord of the church, however, shall continue to endure." These were not merely words, as you know, for Desmond Tutu had to pay a price for his confession. Herein, however, lies the witness of the church. Words alone are no longer important.

In South Africa we are confronted by a choice. Often that choice is obedience to the government or obedience to God. We must receive from God alone the faith and trust and courage to make the right decision. I think that I must tell you that if the churches in South Africa are confronted by a choice, then *you too*, Christians living in the Netherlands, are involved in that choice. No longer is it possible to remain neutral in this issue. Neutrality, as you know, is the most abominable demonstration of partiality because it means choosing the side of power and injustice without assuming responsibility for them. This you can no longer do. You, too, must make a choice. Make that choice in the framework of your political, economic, and cultural responsibility here in the Netherlands, in the framework of your ecumenical responsibility in the church, and in the framework of your responsibility relative to your sister churches in South Africa who rely on you, who hope in you, and who wait on your intercession.

May I conclude by telling you what we in South Africa earnestly desire from you? I hope that I do not ask too much of you. We ask you to take seriously the WARC decision in your own consultations and decision-making processes. We ask you also to take WARC seriously as an instrument by which we may tell the world where we, in South Africa, stand. The Nederduits Gereformeerde Mission Church, of which I am a member and a minister, has come so far that last year, in our synod, we said that we had discovered that we cannot continue to exist as church in South Africa if we did not continue to exist as a confessing church. Therefore, we have written our own confession. We did not do this for the purpose of adding another confession to all the already existing confessions. We did it, rather, to state explicitly to the government, to the world, and also to ourselves, where we stand relative to situations of political, economic, and social conflict and oppression.

We ask you to join us as we, together, are and remain the church of the Lord, the Body of Christ. It is very important that we hold on to this organic identity. This we are for the benefit of one another. Why does Paul take such pains to remind the church that if one member suffers, all the other members suffer? We cannot forget the solidarity that we have with one another simply because our problems are not your problems—at least not immediately and directly.

In this context we request you to support us through your support of the ecumenical movement; above all, by your support of the WCC Program to Combat Racism. We request that you support us directly as churches in South Africa related to you in the WCC, and as churches related to you in WARC.

Often it is difficult for us. I request that you, therefore, pray for us. In South Africa we often are confronted with the temptation to skirt problems when we know that an explicitly stated point of view relative to those problems may result in persecution; to remain silent in the face of certain problems; to speak ambiguously about certain problems or to do nothing in response to something that will anger the government. We have discovered, however, that if we act in these ways we abandon one another and become unfaithful to the gospel.

We request you to pray that we shall always be faithful to the gospel. Although it is true that we at times are fearful, and although it is true that we at times wish we did not need to speak out, we ask you in your private prayer and in your solidarity with us to pray that the churches in South Africa may remain faithful, that they may persevere in faith so that the word of the Lord may remain a living word and may maintain its healing power in South Africa.

Pray also that we do not surrender to the hate that often wells up within us. It is not always easy in South Africa, in the midst of oppression and violence, of discrimination and dehumanization, to maintain respect for the humanity of others. In such circumstances, moreover, to discuss dispassionately over a cup of coffee the real meaning of "tolerance" is impossible. Often, despite the objections of our own mind and conscience, hate overwhelms us. This I experienced myself, in 1980, when the police shot and killed the first boy, Bernard Fortuin, in Elsiesriver near Capetown. The story appeared in all the newspapers. Bernard Fortuin was lying on the street, bleeding to death. His mother ran from the house. She wished to be by her son during the last moments of his life. The police, however, drove her away with their guns. One screamed at her, "Let the bastard die!" At a time like that you think to yourself that it would be good if, only for a moment, you could have revenge, so that you could rid yourself of the pain that fills your heart. But by the same token you know that if we in South Africa build our future on hatred and revenge, then all is lost. We ask for your prayer and your support so that hatred and the desire for revenge do not overwhelm us; that would be fatal.

The WARC decision has given us hope. In this hope we wish to move forward. We know that we cannot do this alone. Therefore we ask you to accompany us on the road ahead. It will not be easy for you. The choice to do so or not to do so, however, must be made. If the Lord himself has made the choice, then we and you also must make the choice.

Chapter XIII

"Where Is Your Brother . . .?" (Genesis 4:9)

I should like to reflect on the story of Cain and Abel in Genesis 4:1–17. The first point I wish to make is that we ought not to regard the story of Cain and Abel as a story about two persons who lived a long time ago when everything was much more primitive than it is today, in comparison with whom, we are much more cultivated and civilized. After one has read this story one should not say that it is good that we today are no longer like Cain and Abel.

The story of Cain and Abel is a story about two types or kinds of persons. It is a very human story that is still being enacted today. This story does not tell us in the first place what happened once upon a time; rather, it tells us about something that happens today. Because this story is a human story, we find very human elements in it and elements from our own human history. On the one hand, it is a depressing story; on the other hand, it is a hopeful story.

"Cain"—in Hebrew, *kayin*, "smith"—is the maker, the creator, the strong one, the leader. At Cain's birth, his mother makes an announcement: "With the help of God I have received a man-child." With pride she informs the world of this event. When Abel is born, nothing is said; he is born without announcement.

This sermon was preached by Dr. Boesak on Sunday, June 5, 1983, in the New Remonstrant Church, Amsterdam, the Netherlands.

"Abel" (perhaps derived from the Hebrew *hebel*, "nothingness") is a breath or wind, like the morning mist or fog that is quickly driven away by the rising sun. That is what happens to him. In a few verses he disappears. In this story, then, there is a younger brother, a smaller and weaker brother; and a stronger brother, the ruler, the creator.

What was Cain's responsibility with respect to his brother Abel? He did not have the responsibility to be Abel's keeper. Neither was his responsibility to be Abel's ruler. Nor was he Abel's guardian. His responsibility, rather, was to be Abel's brother. This responsibility involves being human in community with one another in God's world. It means to seek together for true humanity; to attempt together to make something of God's objectives visibly operative in the world; to let something of God's own heart become visible in fraternal relationships; and, in a corporate relationship in history, to humanize the world and keep it humanized. This is what it means to be a brother.

Cain rejects this human responsibility in the most abominable manner: he murders his brother. The author time after time underlines the fact that Cain and Abel were brothers. We are not to forget that they were brothers. The story does not focus merely on a crime, but on the most heinous crime. Cain did not kill some anonymous person; he murdered his own brother. The story states emphatically that Cain said to his *brother* Abel, "Let us go into the field." When they arrived in the field, Cain rose up against his *brother* Abel and killed him. And the Lord said to Cain, "Where is your *brother* Abel?" Make no mistake about it; pay attention, people of God: This story concerns the core of our humanity.

Then you hear Cain's answer. It sounds sarcastic. God asks Cain, "Where is your brother?" Cain answers, "My goodness! I don't know! Am I my brother's keeper?" There is some mockery in his answer. Cain was a farmer, and Abel was a keeper, a herdsman of small animals—sheep and goats. He was a keeper. Cain asks God, "Am I the herdsman of the herdsman?" But God does not share Cain's humor, for the matter at hand is very serious. It involves life and death.

God then makes Cain's punishment known. That punishment

interests us. In that day, after all, human beings were much more primitive than we are. The idea of blood vengeance, however, does not function here. Cain was not hung on a gallows. He was not placed before a firing squad. He was not executed. He is allowed to live on. Of this he receives a sign from God. He becomes, however, a pilgrim on the earth, a wanderer. He must go and live in the land of Nod. Cain was very frightened. He said to God, "Why do you do this to me? My punishment is too heavy to bear!" We moderns, in amazement, want to ask Cain, "Why are you so frightened? Aren't you happy that you can live? It's certainly better to wander on the face of the earth than to die immediately, isn't it?"

Cain knows, however, what it means that he no longer fits in with the land. He does not belong there now. He is a farmer. The whole of his life and all his hope is bound up with the land. He finds his joy in the land. When he exerts himself, when he uses his strength, then something comes up out of the earth. The fruit of his work becomes tangible. He may taste it. He may share that fruit with others. That is meaningful. That is a legitimate human satisfaction, is it not? Now Cain must leave all this. He no longer possesses the land. He must go and live in the land of Nod.

Where is the land of Nod? Nod is "east of Eden"—that is, away from the land that God had designated as the place where Cain and Abel were to live human lives, where they were to be men, brothers, real persons. Eden was the place, the garden, where true humanity was born; where God brought persons together; where God said, "Here, together, in community, we begin human history." Now Cain may not live there. Cain is, as it were, out of bounds. He is far from the place where real life is. He is in the land of Nod.

Cain comes under a curse. The earth can no longer be fruitful for him. It is, after all, the same earth that opened its mouth and drank the blood of Abel, his brother. Therefore, the earth can no longer bear fruit for him. The earth mourns. The earth chokes in blood and cannot respond to Cain. The earth can no longer converse with him. The earth can no longer return anything to him. Cain's relationship to the land is ruptured. It no longer exists. It has been bloodied.

Cain comes under a second curse. He must be a wanderer, a vagabond, in the world. Nod is a "state of mind" in which one wanders forever. Cain must live as someone who has no goal. Never again will he be at rest. Never again will there be fixed ground, a known place, beneath his feet. Never again will there be a place where he belongs, where he is at home.

What does that mean for us? I think that the story is meant to tell us that oppressors shall have no place on God's earth. Oppressors have no home. Oppressors do not belong to, are not at home in, God's objectives for this world. They have gone out of bounds. They have removed themselves from the world. Cain broke not only his relationship to the land, but also his relationship to God. Because Abel is no longer there, there is no longer a relationship to God. This is what the story says. When Abel no longer lives and Cain is "brotherless," then Cain immediately is "Godless." "Look," he says, "you hide your face from me. You send me from your presence." Oppressors have no place, no rest for their souls.

When I lived in the Netherlands, I became acquainted with all sorts of proverbs. The English say, "Fortune favors the bold." The Dutch version of this proverb reads, "The bold have half the world." That proverb may be true, yet something must be said about it. It is one thing to claim the earth for one's self by violent means; it is quite a different thing to verify Jesus' saying, "The meek shall inherit the earth." There is a great difference between these two. The difference lies in this: according to God's objective or purpose, the violent have no place in God's world, try as they may, with violence, to possess God's world.

This brings up a second, related matter: those who take another's life can never again be certain about their own life. They continue to wonder when the hour of vengeance will toll for them. If I cause another to suffer, when will that violence be reciprocated as vengeance? Because of this, dear brothers and sisters, the violent and oppressive are very anxious, uncertain, frightened persons. They live in anxiety and fear because they are the constant cause of anxiety and fear in others. They must live with their own conscience. They do not sleep well. It may appear that they do, but that appearance is deceptive. They do not have rest for their souls.

I could give countless illustrations of this from South Africa. Our government can be called the most powerful military government on the continent of Africa. And so frequently on the Afrikaner television we can see tanks and all sorts of weapons that have been developed by the astute in Pretoria or elsewhere. These weapons systems are paraded back and forth to frighten and intimidate everyone. Who, however, are the most frightened? You cannot prosper from oppression; you can only die from it.

There is no hope in oppression, no openness and no future. Reflect on a hypothetical example. I make a law to the effect that two persons who love one another may not marry if they are racially diverse. For this reason and no other, the two may not marry. Suppose I have a daughter who falls in love with a person of the "wrong" color and wishes to marry! You can never be certain that it will not happen! Think of the anxiety this causes.

Reflect on another hypothetical example: I make a law that only blacks who have working permits may live in certain areas of the land. All other blacks, including the wives and children of those who have working permits, must reside in areas designated for them by the government and euphemistically called "homelands." If a black wife goes with her children to live as a family with her husband, the children's father, she violates my law and is liable to deportation to her designated "homeland." I have made a law that makes it impossible for blacks to live together as a family. At the same time, as a Christian, I confess that the family is sacred, that God wills that husband and wife live together. What God has brought together, my law puts asunder.

Suppose that tomorrow the roles were reversed. Suppose that tomorrow or the day after there were to be a black government that did not remove all the apartheid laws, that left them all in effect, with the roles of black and white reversed, including the designation of "homelands" for the whites. Suppose we began to shoot at the whites. What would happen? The most anxious persons in South Africa in that hypothetical situation would be the blacks. They would live in anxiety because they would never know what might happen the next moment. The really frightened ones, who are eaten up by anxiety, are those who think that peace lies in the insecurity and oppression of the other; those who think that peace lies in the ability to destroy the other, to take the life of the other; those who think that to intimidate the other and to threaten the death of the other constitutes their own security and certainty.

South Africans, of course, are not the only ones who are guilty of locating and defining their peace and security erroneously, and who, consequently, suffer great anxiety. Everywhere there are those who insist that what is necessary for our security is nuclear weapons. They insist that if the Russians develop missile delivery systems that will enable them to destroy the earth not fifty-two times over, such as those we now possess, but fifty-six times, then the Western powers must develop missile delivery systems that can destroy the earth sixty-three times over! And if the Russians develop missiles that can strike New York in two minutes—or, as a result of a mistake, Amsterdam—then the Western powers must develop missiles that can strike Moscow in thirty seconds. When we have planned these new weapons and delivery systems, then we shall devote billions of dollars to their production, and we shall say, "Oh, how blessed we are, for we now have peace and security!"

How we do inflict pain upon ourselves! How we inflict pain upon God's people! Do we think that security lies in violence? The violent are not only those who pick up guns; the violent are also those who protect those who pick up guns, who encourage them, who aid them, and speak well of them.

You ought not to think that you are safer in Amsterdam than in South Africa, or that you are farther from evil here than there. Sin lies—this is what God tells Cain—directly in front of your door, and it desires to capture you. It does not lie far from Pretoria; it lies directly in front of the door.

Cain continues to live. He continues to live, I suspect, to make it clear that his type of life—a life of restlessness, uneasiness, uncertainty, violence, ceaseless wandering, a life in which there is no peace with God and one's fellows—is not what is intended for those who earnestly seek God.

There is a second reason why Cain remains alive: God gives Cain an opportunity to ask for forgiveness. Does God forgive murderers? Yes, of course! God does that! Nowhere is this better illustrated than in the life of Jesus of Nazareth. Next to Jesus, as he hangs on the cross, there hangs a murderer. He turns to Jesus. He knows all about confession of sin. He knows about sorrow. He knows about asking for forgiveness. He knows about turning to God. And he does so. What happens? He is forgiven. If Cain the murderer is driven from the land, the murderer on the cross receives the promise of paradise. That is the difference that Jesus of Nazareth makes.

History moves on. Does Cain's generation learn anything? Does it improve? Or do we learn, rather, that Cain's generation cannot change, cannot improve? It seems that things cannot change. A little later we read the story of Lamech. Lamech said to his wives Ada and Zillah:

> Listen to me:
> I have killed a young man
> because he struck me.
> If seven lives are taken to pay
> for killing Cain,
> seventy-seven will be taken if
> anyone kills Lamech [Gen. 5:23–24].

There are still "wise guys" among us; the ruffians still have the last word; the powerful continue to do the talking. The question is: Shall we ever escape the circle of violence, anger, anxiety, and restlessness? Here, again, you can see what a difference Jesus of Nazareth makes in human history: the words of Lamech are reversed by Jesus. Lamech says that he will be avenged seventy-seven times over. But Jesus tells his followers to forgive others, not seventy-seven times, but seventy times seven times. It is, therefore, possible, Jesus tells us, to break the vicious circle. It is possible to transcend the normal human niveau, to achieve the unusual in our own life. It is possible to transcend blood, revenge, violence, and murder, anxiety and uncertainty.

Is it possible to transcend our present situation in South Africa? Can it still happen? I do not know. I do not know how to tell blacks in South Africa to forgive seventy times seven times—

those who have seen their own children shot and killed in the streets. I do not know how to tell them this. I do not know how to tell Mrs. Fortuin, who in Capetown in 1980 was prevented by the police from attending her son, Bernard, who had been shot by the police and lay dying on the street. What does one say to her? What can I say about forgiveness to those who know that their son who was born in one of the homelands in South Africa will never see his first birthday because he will die before then from kwashiorkor, or malnutrition, or starvation? What can I say about forgiveness to those who one morning, unexpectedly, are informed that they are no longer South African citizens because the government arbitrarily has assigned them to one of the homelands? What can one say about forgiveness to older persons who are forcibly expelled from their homes in a heavy-handed and forceful way; and are thrown into a relocation camp where they may well perish, finally, from starvation and sorrow?

We ought not to speak too hastily about forgiveness and similar matters. And yet—we read these words of the Lord, words that we cannot avoid. Ought we to believe that what is impossible for us is possible for God? With God all things are possible, including forgiveness welling up out of the hearts of suffering and oppressed black South Africans. That too. Precisely that.

The story of Cain ends with the report of a joyful event. Adam and Eve have another son. His name is Seth. Eve says, "God has given me another son in the place of Abel whom Cain killed." She does not repudiate history. She does not bypass this tragic event as if it had not happened. She does not ignore reality. She knows this, only this: with this child God wishes to begin all over again with her—and therefore also with all other persons. The story ends not in tragedy but in words of hope: "At that time men began to call upon the name of the Lord" (Gen. 5:26). After murder, after death, after annihilation and inhumanity, God begins again.

There is a little-known play of the Dutch playwright, Jan Wolkers, entitled *Closed because of Death.* In this play Wolkers tells us how history finally ends. Everyone dies. The earth once more is desolate and uninhabited. Perhaps we humans shall finally be successful in bringing about what we try so hard to do with our nuclear weapons! Not one person remains on the earth.

At this point in the play, the scene shifts to heaven. God is sitting there with a little monkey on his knee. He caresses the monkey, and he plays with the monkey. He stares off into the distance, and the audience is able to understand what God is thinking about.

Two angels walk by. The one says to the other, "Oh, oh! Do you see what I see?"

"Yes!" says the second angel. "Do you think that I am thinking what he is thinking?"

"Yes!" says the first angel, "I am afraid I do."

Then as God is stroking the rib cage of the monkey, the angels become terribly excited, and the one says anxiously to the other, "What's he going to do to us now? He isn't going to start all over again, is he? Doesn't he ever learn? He can see for himself what's going to happen! He's already learned that it doesn't work! And then to start all over again—that can't be!"

The second angel says, reflectively and somberly, "That's precisely the difference between him and us. He always sees a chance to start all over again."

That, brothers and sisters, is, I think, the most hopeful word in the gospel of Jesus Christ. After oppression, murder, terror, inhumanity, apartheid, and the gobbling up of the profits of apartheid, and finally death—after all this, God still wishes to begin all over again with us. Look at the life, death, and resurrection of Jesus Christ. When he was going through this oppression and, finally, death, he clung to the hope that illuminates the human story: "If God will. . . ."

If God wishes to start all over again with us in the resurrection of Jesus, that is God's insurrection against evil, disobedience, violence, murder—against sin. In 1983, in Jesus Christ, our story can be transformed and converted so that in the final analysis it is evident as the human story, the story that ends as God planned it to end.

Chapter XIV

Jesus Christ, the Life of the World

Jesus Christ the life of the world! These are words that speak of joy, of meaning, of hope. For some, they may even speak of triumph and victory. These are words that have a ring of certainty in them. Yet, in the uncertain world of suffering, oppression, and death, what do they mean? The realities of the world in which we live suggest the cold grip of death rather than the vibrant freedom of life.

Violence, greed, and the demonic distortion of human values continue to destroy God's world and God's people. Economic exploitation is escalating rather than abating, and economic injustice is still the dominant reality in the relationships between rich and poor countries. Racism is as rampant as ever, not only in South Africa, but also in other parts of the world. In its alliances with national security ideologies, racism has acquired a new cloak of respectability and has become even more pervasive. In South Africa apartheid and injustice still reign supreme. Inequality is still sanctified by law, and racial superiority is still justified by theology. Today, with the blatant support of many Western governments, apartheid seems stronger than ever, and the dream of justice and human dignity for South African blacks seems more remote than ever.

This address was delivered at the sixth assembly of the World Council of Churches in Vancouver, British Columbia, Canada, in July 1983.

In our world it is not the joyful, hopeful sound of the word of life that is being heard. No, that word is drowned by the ugly sound of gunfire, by the screams of our children, and by the endless cry of the powerless: "How long, Lord?"

In too many places too many children die of hunger, and too many persons just disappear because they dare to stand up for justice and human rights. Too many are swept away by the tides of war, and too many are tortured in dungeons of death. In too many eyes the years of endless struggle have extinguished the fires of hope and joy, and too many bodies are bowed down by the weight of that peculiarly repugnant death called despair. Too many young persons believe that their youth and their future are already powdered to dust by the threat of nuclear destruction. And even in the face of all this, too many in the Christian church remain silent. We have not yet understood that every act of inhumanity, every unjust law, every untimely death, every utterance of confidence in weapons of mass destruction, every justification of violence and oppression, is a sacrifice on the altar of the false gods of death; it is a denial of the Lord of life. For millions it is true: we are not uplifted by the word of life, we are crushed by the litany of death.

Yet the gospel affirms: Jesus Christ is the life of the world (John 6:35, 48; 10:10; 11:25; 14:6; Rev. 1:17, 18, etc.). This means he is the source of life; he is the giver of the sacred gift of life. He intends for us a life filled with abundance, joy, and meaning. He is the Messiah in whose eyes our lives are precious.

This affirmation is precisely the problem. Dare we believe it? Can we believe it without making of our faith a narrow, spiritual escapism? Can we avoid the cynicism of "reality"? Can we find a way to live with that painful dilemma: "Lord, I believe; please help my unbelief"? And even more painful: can we accept the reality of hope and the call to battle that lie in this affirmation? In other words, is the joyous affirmation, this confession that Jesus Christ is the life of the world, really meant for the millions who suffer and die, who are oppressed and who live without hope in the world today? When discussing this theme with a group in my congregation, a woman once said quietly, almost despairingly: "It seems you have to be white and rich to believe this."

There are two things we must remember when talking about this confession. First, in the gospel this affirmation is never a triumphalistic banzai. It is never a slogan built on might and power. It is a confession in the midst of weakness, suffering, and death. It is the quiet piety that the Christian church cannot do without. Secondly, we must be reminded that in the Bible this affirmation is given to those who in their situation *were* the poor, oppressed, and weak. They were the ones who lived on the underside of history. And it is *they* who are called upon to confirm this truth: Jesus Christ is the life of the world.

In the fourth chapter of St. John the story of Jesus and the Samaritan woman is a good illustration of this truth. She is the paradigm par excellence of the despised, the weak, and the oppressed, just as children are elsewhere in the gospels. She becomes the very example of the dejected of this world. First of all, she is a woman, with all that that means in the society of her day. Notice how John makes a point of stating the disciples' astonishment that Jesus was in discussion with a woman. She is also a Samaritan, and therefore despised and rejected by the Jews. Her religion is considered inferior. In her own community she is an outcast because of her way of life. This is probably the reason why she goes to that well alone, at a most unusual hour of the day. But it is precisely to her that Jesus speaks of these unfathomable things: the life-giving waters, and the waters of life.

Likewise, the Apocalypse of John is written to a weak, scattered underground church, suffering severely under the persecution of a ruthless tyrant. The followers of Jesus had no recourse, no protection under the law, no "connections" in high and powerful places, no political or economic power. Their lives were cheap. They were completely and utterly surrendered to the mercy of a man who did not know the meaning of the words "surrender" and "mercy," whom John could describe only with the telling title: "beast." From a purely human point of view, they had not a chance in the world. There was precious little upon which they could build their hopes for the future. But like the Samaritan woman, *they* are those who hear the message: "I am the first and the last and the living one. . . ." They knew with a certainty not born of earthly power: Jesus Christ, not the Caesar (in spite of all *his* power!), is the life of the world. The imperial claims of divinity, of immortality, of omniscience and power are the lies, the half-truths, the propaganda without which no tyrant can survive. But the truth stands: Jesus Christ is the life of the world; indeed he is the Lord of life.

The church understood this confession not only as comfort in times of trial and darkness, but as an essential part of that basic confession: Jesus Christ is Lord. In this way this confession became not only comfort to the persecuted, oppressed church, but also a ringing protest against the arrogance of earthly potentates who wanted desperately to create the impression that *they* decided over the life and death of the people of God. And the church knew this confession to be the truth, not only for the life hereafter, but the truth for the very life and the very world in which they struggled to believe, to be faithful, to be obedient. To understand that is to understand the power—nay more, to experience the power—of the life-giving Word. It is to drink of the life-giving and living waters even when one is faced with suffering, destruction, and death. It is to understand and experience what it means to worship.

This worship is not confined to certain moments only. It is a worship that encompasses all of our life, so that every prayer for liberation, every act for the sake of human dignity, every commitment in the struggle for true human freedom, every protest against the sinful realities of this world becomes an offering to the Living One for the sake of the kingdom.

Jesus says: "The hour comes, and now is." Here the present and the future coincide. The moment of the hesitant, yet faithful human response and the moment of the favor of the Lord come together.

This is the source of the acts of sublime courage which sometimes are displayed in the witness and the life of the Christian church. This is what led to the witness of the Christian church at the martyrdom of St. Polycarp:

> The blessed Polycarp died a martyr's death on the 23rd of February, on the Great Sabbath, the eighth hour. Herod imprisoned him when Phillip of Tralles was the High Priest,

> and Statius Quartus was the Proconsul, whilst for ever is King our Lord Jesus Christ. His be the glory, honor, majesty, and an everlasting throne from generation to generation. Amen.

And indeed it may seem as if for the moment the dictators of this world, the powerful and the mighty, have full control over this world. Their arrogance seems to have no bounds. Their power seems unchecked. But the church knows: Jesus Christ is Lord of history; he is Lord of life; his truth shall have the final word.

In the same way Christians in South Africa are beginning to understand that for us God's moment is brought together with our present reality. We are beginning to discern that the church is called to an extraordinarily courageous witness for the sake of the gospel, such as that of Bishop Desmond Tutu when he said to the South African minister of law and order: "Mr. Minister, we must remind you that you are not God. You are just a man. And one day your name shall merely be a faint scribble on the pages of history, while the name of Jesus Christ, the Lord of the church, shall live forever."

The Christian church can take this stand, not because it possesses earthly power, or because it has "control" over the situation. Over against the political, economic, and military powers that seek to rule this world, the church remains weak and in a sense defenseless. But it takes this stand because it refuses to believe that the powers of oppression, death, and destruction have the last word. Even when facing these powers the church continues to believe that Jesus Christ is Lord and, therefore, the life of the world. And it is this faith in the living One, this refusal to bow down to the false gods of death, that is the strength of the church.

This affirmation has another ramification. Jesus Christ is the life of the *world*. His concern is not only the church but also the world. In his life, death, and resurrection lies not only the future of the church, but the future of the world. In the letter to the Ephesians, Paul is persistent in proclaiming Jesus Christ as Lord of the church and of the cosmos. His being our peace has consequences not only for the church, but also for the world. Therefore the church must proclaim, clearly and unequivocally, that Jesus Christ came to give meaningful life to the world, so that all human history, all human activity, can be renewed and liberated from death and destruction.

The life of the world, the destruction of this world, and the future of this world, are therefore the concern of the church. We have a responsibility for this world for it is God's world. If this world is threatened by the evils of militarism, materialism, greed, racism, it is very much the concern of the church. The church has heard these words: "Today I am giving you a choice between good and evil, between life and death . . . choose life!" And the church has heard these words: "I have come so that they may have life . . . abundantly." And because we have heard this, and because we confess Jesus Christ as the life of the world, we dare not be silent.

This assembly of the World Council of Churches must speak out. We must confess humbly, and without any hesitation, our faith in Jesus Christ, the life of the world. We must humbly, and without any hesitation, renew our commitment to Jesus Christ, the life of the world. And this faith, this commitment, must be the basis of our action on the issues of peace, justice, and human liberation. We must not hesitate to address ourselves to the question of peace and to the possibility of total nuclear destruction. We must be clear: the nuclear arms race, the employment of God-given human talents and possibilities for the creation of more refined weapons of mass destruction, and the call to put our faith in these weapons to secure our peace, is not simply a temporary madness; it is essentially sinful and contrary to the purposes of God for this world and for humankind.

I am not persuaded that the issue of peace is simply one of fashion, a fad that will die out tomorrow. I do not agree with those who believe that this issue is simply one of political and military calculations, so that the church should withdraw from the debate and let the problems be solved by the politicians and the military strategists. I remain convinced that the issue of peace as it faces us today lies at the very heart of the gospel.

When the World Alliance of Reformed Churches met in Ottawa last August, we spent considerable time discussing a statement on peace. During the debate, a delegate from Africa made a remark that very poignantly raised some of the tensions surrounding this issue in the ecumenical movement today. He said: "In this document, the word 'nuclear' is used a number of times, but I don't even see the word 'hunger.' In my village, the people will not understand the word 'nuclear,' but they know everything about hunger and poverty."

What he was talking about was the concern of many Christians in the Third World that the issue of peace will be separated from the issue of justice, making of "peace" primarily a North Atlantic concern. This should not happen, first of all, because ideologies of militarism and national security are international in character and cause deprivation and the continuation of injustice everywhere, but especially in the so-called Third World countries. Secondly, and more importantly, in the Bible peace and justice are never separated. Peace is never simply the absence of war; it is the active presence of justice. It has to do with human fulfillment, with liberation, with wholeness, with a meaningful life and well-being not only for individuals, but for the community as a whole. The prophet Isaiah speaks of peace as the offshoot of justice.

It may be true that the issues of justice, racism, hunger, and poverty are largely unresolved issues in the ecumenical movement. It may be true that these issues present the churches with painful dilemmas, but we cannot be willing to use the issue of peace to avoid those dilemmas. One cannot use the gospel to escape the demands of the gospel. And one cannot use the issue of peace to escape the unresolved issues of injustice, poverty, hunger, and racism. If we did this, we would be making of our concern for peace an ideology of oppression that in the end would be used to justify injustice.

Jesus Christ is the life of the world because he reveals the truth about himself, the church, humankind, and the world. He is the Messiah, the chosen of God who proclaims the acceptable year of the Lord. In him is the fulfillment of the promises of Yahweh. He is the Servant of the Lord who shall not cease his struggle until justice triumphs on the earth (Isa. 42:1–3; Matt. 12:17–32). In him shall the nations place their hope.

Jesus, in his life, death, and resurrection, is himself the guarantee of life, peace, and human dignity. He is the Messiah who struggles and suffers with his people, and, yet, he is the victor. He is king in his suffering; not in spite of it. There is therefore an inseparable link between Pontius Pilate's "Ecce homo!" and his "There is your King!" (John 19:4, 19). The Apocalypse speaks of Jesus both as the Lamb that was slaughtered and also as the Rider on the white horse. The one who died is the one who lives forever. The suffering Servant of the world is the ruler of the kings of the earth. The one who was willing to give up his life is Jesus the Messiah, the life of the world. This is the truth that is revealed to the church even as we speak the words: Jesus Christ is the life of the world. The Revelation of John reminds us of the victory of the saints. Again, it is not a victory brought about by earthly powers: "They won the victory [over Satan] by the blood of the Lamb, and by the truth they proclaimed, and because they did not love their life unto death" (Rev. 12:11). This truth is the basis upon which the church stands. It is the essence of the witness of the church in the world. It is the essence of the confession: Jesus Christ is the life of the world. The church can say this only if we are willing to give our life for the sake of the world. We can say this only if we truly believe that there are some things so dear, some things so precious, some things so eternally true that they are worth dying for. And the truth that Jesus Christ is the life of the world is worth giving our life for.

The truth that the Messiah reveals is contrary to the lies, the propaganda, the idolatry, the untrustworthiness in the world. His truth is the truth that contains the freedom and the life of the world. This truth we are called to proclaim. As the assembled churches of the world, let us affirm this truth, and let us believe:

> It is not true that this world and its inhabitants are doomed to die and be lost.
> *This* is true: For God so loved the world that he gave his only begotten Son, that whosoever believes in him shall not perish, but have everlasting life.

It is not true that we must accept inhumanity and discrimination, hunger and poverty, death and destruction.
This is true: I have come that they may have life, and that abundantly.

It is not true that violence and hatred shall have the last word, and that war and destruction have come to stay forever.
This is true: For unto us a child is born, and unto us a Son is given, and the government shall be upon his shoulder, and his name shall be called wonderful counselor, mighty God, the everlasting Father, the Prince of peace.

It is not true that we are simply victims of the powers of evil that seek to rule the world.
This is true: To me is given all authority in heaven and on earth, and lo, I am with you always, even unto the end of the world.

It is not true that we have to wait for those who are specially gifted, who are the prophets of the church, before we can do anything.
This is true: I will pour out my Spirit on all flesh, and your sons and your daughters shall prophesy, your young men shall see visions, and your old men shall have dreams.

It is not true that our dreams for the liberation of humankind, our dreams of justice, of human dignity, of peace, are not meant for this earth and for this history.
This is true: The hour comes, and it is now, that true worshipers shall worship the Father in spirit and in truth.

So, let us dream. Let us prophesy! Let us see visions of love, and peace, and justice. Let us affirm with humility, with joy, with faith, with courage: *Jesus Christ is the life of the world*.

Chapter XV

Peace in Our Day

We have arrived at a historic moment. We have now brought together under the aegis of the United Democratic Front the broadest and most significant coalition of groups and organizations struggling against apartheid, racism, and injustice in South Africa since the early 1950s. We have been able to create a unity among freedom-loving persons that this country has not seen for many a year.

I am particularly happy to note that this meeting is not merely a gathering of isolated individuals. No, we represent organizations deeply rooted in the struggle for justice, deeply rooted in the heart of our people. Indeed, I believe we are standing at the birth of what could become the greatest and most significant popular movement in more than a quarter of a century.

We are here to say that the constitutional proposals of the government are inadequate, and that they do not express the will of the vast majority of South Africans. But more than that, we are here to say that what we are working for is one, undivided South Africa that shall belong to all its people: an open democracy from which no South African shall be excluded; a society in which the human dignity of all shall be respected. We are here to say that there are rights that are neither conferred by nor derived from the

This address was delivered at the national launching of the United Democratic Front, Cape Town, South Africa, on August 20, 1983.

state; you have to go back beyond the dim mist of eternity to understand their origin: they are God-given. And we are not here to beg for those rights; we are here to claim them.

In a sense, the formation of the United Democratic Front both highlights and symbolizes the crisis that apartheid and its supporters have created for themselves. After a history of some three hundred thirty years of slavery, racial discrimination, dehumanization, and economic exploitation, what the supporters of apartheid expected was acceptance of the status quo, docility, and subservience. Instead they are finding persons who refuse to accept racial injustice, and who are ready to face the challenges of the moment.

After more than three decades of apartheid, the supporters of apartheid expected humble submission to the harsh rule of totalitarianism and racial supremacy. Instead, they are finding persons who are ready to fight this evil system at every level of society.

After more than twenty years of apartheid education, the supporters of apartheid expected to see totally brainwashed, perfect little *hotnotjies* and *kaffertjies* who knew their place in the world. Instead, they are finding the most politically conscious generation of young persons determined to struggle for a better future.

After the draconian measures of the 1960s and the ever harsher oppression of the so-called security laws, the supporters of apartheid expected a people immobilized by the tranquilizing drugs of apathy and fear. Instead, they faced a rising tide of political and human consciousness that swept away complacency and shook South Africa to its very foundations.

After the tragic happenings of the 1970s—the banning of our organizations and of so many of those who struggled for justice, the torture and death of so many in detention, the merciless killing of our children on the streets of the nation—the supporters of apartheid expected surrender. Instead, here we are at this historic occasion telling South Africa and the world: we are struggling for our human dignity and for the future of our children! We will never give up!

Those in power in this country have made the fundamental mistake of all totalitarian regimes that depend not on the loyalty of the people but on the power of the gun: they have not reckoned with the determination of a people to be free. Those in power depend on propaganda, deceit, and coercion. They have forgotten that no lie can live forever, and that the fear of the gun is always overcome by the longing for freedom. They have forgotten that you can kill the body but you cannot kill the spirit and the determination of a people.

The immediate reason for our coming together today is the continuation of the apartheid policies of the government as seen in the constitutional proposals. In recent weeks some persons have asked me with greater urgency than before: "Why do you not see the positive side of apartheid?"

When you are white, your children's education is guaranteed and paid for by the state. When your job is secure and blacks are prevented from being too competitive, when your home and property have never been confiscated by the government, and citizenship in the country of your birth is not in danger, when your children do not have to die of hunger and malnutrition and your privileged position in society is guaranteed by security laws and the best equipped army on the African continent—then I can understand why some believe that apartheid has its positive side.

For those of us, however, who are black and who suffer under this system there is no positive side to apartheid. How can we see something positive in a system built on oppression, injustice, and exploitation? What is positive about a system that systematically and deliberately destroys human dignity, that makes a criterion as irrelevant and unimportant as skin color the basis of society and the key to the understanding of human relationships, political participation, and economic justice? How can apartheid be positive when in the name of Christianity it spawns policies that cause little children to die of hunger and malnutrition, that break up black family life and spell out a continuous, hopeless death for millions of blacks?

How can apartheid be positive when it keeps most South African children manacled in the chains of unfreedom and the others manacled in the chains of fear? The time has come for white South Africans to realize that their destiny is inextricably bound up with our destiny, and that they shall never be free until we are free. How happy I am that many of our white brothers and sisters are saying this by their presence here today.

Those who think their security and peace lie in the perpetuation of intimidation, dehumanization, and violence are *not* free. They will never be free as long as they have to kill our children in order to safeguard their overprivileged positions. They will never be free as long as they have to lie awake at night wondering if, when white power will have come to its inevitable end, a black government will do the same to them as they now are doing to us.

We must also ask the question: What is positive about the new constitutional proposals of the government? In order that there should be no misunderstanding, let me, as clearly and briefly as possible, repeat the reasons why we reject these proposals:

1) Racism, so embedded in South African society, is once again written into the constitution. All over the world, persons are beginning to recognize that racism is politically untenable, sociologically unsound, and morally unacceptable. In this country, however, the doctrine of racial supremacy, although condemned by most churches in South Africa as heresy and idolatry, is once again enshrined in the constitution as the basis upon which to build the further development of our society and the nurturing of human relationships.

2) All the basic laws, those that are the very pillars of apartheid, and without which the system cannot survive—laws concerning mixed marriages, group areas, racial classification, separate and unequal education—remain untouched and unchanged by the new proposals.

3) The homelands policy, which is surely the most immoral and objectionable aspect of the apartheid policies of the government, forms the basis of the willful exclusion of 80 percent of our nation from the new political deal. Indeed, in the words of the President's Council, the homelands policy is to be regarded as "irreversible." So our black African brothers and sisters will be driven even further into the wilderness of homeland politics. Millions will have to find their political rights in the sham independence of those bush republics. Millions more will continue to lose their South African citizenship, and millions more will be removed forcibly from their homes into resettlement camps.

4) Clearly the oppression will continue; the brutal breakup of black family life will not end. The apartheid line is not at all abolished; it is simply shifted so as to include the so-called coloureds and Indians who are willing to cooperate with the government.

5) Not only is the present system of apartheid given more elasticity, making fundamental change even harder than before, but in the new proposals the dream of democracy for which we strive is still further eroded.

6) Whereas, then, the proposals may mean something for those middle-class blacks who think that the improvement of their own economic position is the highest good, they will not bring any significant changes to the life of those who have no rights at all, who must languish in the poverty and utter destitution of the homelands, and who are forbidden by law to live together as families in what is called "white South Africa."

It cannot be repeated often enough that all South Africans who love this country and who care for its future—black and white, Jew and Gentile, Christian and Muslim—have no option but to reject these proposals.

Apartheid is a cancer in the body politic of the world, a scourge on our society, and an everlasting shame to the church of Jesus Christ in the world and in this country. It exists only because of economic greed, cultural chauvinism, and political oppression maintained by both systemic and physical violence, and a false sense of racial superiority. Therefore we must resist apartheid. We must resist it because it is in fundamental opposition to the noble principles of our Judeo-Christian heritage, and of the Muslim faith. We must resist it because it is a fundamental denial of all that is worthwhile and human in our society. It is in opposition to the will of God for this country. We must resist it because in its claim to be Christian apartheid is blasphemy, idolatry, and heresy.

To be sure, the new proposals will make apartheid less blatant in some ways. It will be modernized and streamlined, and in its new multicolored cloak it will be less conspicuous and less offensive to some. Nonetheless, it will still be there. Apartheid, we must remember, is a thoroughly evil system, and, as such, it cannot be modified, modernized, or steamlined. It has to be eradicated irrevocably. We must continue, therefore, to struggle until that glorious day dawns when apartheid will exist no more.

To those who ask why we are not satisfied and when we shall be satisfied, we must say in clear, patient terms: we shall not be satisfied as long as injustice reigns supreme on the throne of our land. We shall not be satisfied as long as those who rule us are not inspired by justice, but dictated to by fear, greed, and racism. We shall not be satisfied until South Africa is once again one, undivided country, a democracy where there will be meaningful participation in a democratic process of government for all the people. We shall not be satisfied until the wealth and riches of this country are shared by all. We shall not be satisfied until justice rolls down like a waterfall and righteousness like a mighty stream.

There is another important question—namely, that of whites and blacks working together. This has been mentioned as a reason why the United Democratic Front has been so severely attacked by some and why some blacks have refused to cooperate with it. These persons tell us that whites cannot play a meaningful role in the struggle for justice in this country because they are always, by definition, the oppressor. Because the oppression of our people wears a white face, because the laws are made under a system created and maintained by whites, the blacks who attack the United Democratic Front say that there can be no cooperation between whites and blacks until all of this is changed.

To those who think this way I should like to say that I understand the way they feel. We have seen with our own eyes the brutalization of our people at the hands of whites. We have seen police brutality. We have experienced the viciousness and the violence of apartheid. We have been trampled on for so long. For so long we have been dehumanized.

On the other hand we must remember that apartheid does not have the support of *all* whites. There are some who have struggled with us, who have gone to jail, who have been tortured and banned. There have been whites who died in the stuggle for justice. We, therefore, must not allow our anger over apartheid to become the basis for blind hatred of *all* whites. Let us not build our struggle upon hatred; let us not hope for revenge. Let us, even now, seek to lay the foundations for reconciliation between whites and blacks in this country by working together, praying together, struggling together for justice.

The nature and the quality of our struggle for liberation cannot be determined by one's skin color but rather by one's commitment to justice, peace, and human liberation. In the final analysis, judgment will be made not in terms of whiteness or blackness, whatever the ideological content of those words may be today, but in terms of the persistent faithfulness to which we are called in this struggle.

The very fact that we are talking about the constitutional proposals reveals already the paradox in this argument. The government has been pushing ahead with these proposals precisely because they have been supported and accepted by some persons from the black community who think that the short-term economic gains and the semblance of political power are more important than the total liberation of all South Africans. So our struggle is not only against the white government and its plans, but also against those in the black community who through their collaboration give credibility to these plans.

There is something else that must be said. South Africa belongs to all its people. This is a basic truth to which we must cling tenaciously now and in the future. This country is our country. Its future is not safe in the hands of persons, white or black, who despise democracy and trample on the rights of the people. Its future is not safe in the hands of persons, black or white, who to build their empires depend upon economic exploitation and human degradation. Its future is not safe in the hands of persons, black or white, who need the flimsy and deceitful cloak of ethnic superiority to cover the nakedness of their racism. Its future is not safe in the hands of persons, white or black, who seek to secure their unjustly acquired positions of privilege by repressing violently the weak, the exploited, and the needy. Its future is not safe in the hands of persons, white or black, who put their faith simply in the madness of growing militarism. For the sake of our country and our children, therefore, whether *you* be white or black, resist those persons, whether *they* be white or black.

Let us not be fearful of those who sit in the seats of power, whose lips drip with words of interposition and nullification.[1] Let us not be intimidated by those who arrogantly and frighteningly echo their master's voice.

We are doing what we are doing, *not* because we are white or black, but because what we are doing is right. We shall continue so to do until justice and peace embrace, and South Africa becomes the nation it is meant to be.

And as we struggle let us remember that change does not roll in on the wheels of inevitability. It comes through the tireless efforts and hard work of those who are willing to take the risk of fighting for freedom, democracy, and human dignity.

As we struggle on, let us continue to sing that wonderful hymn of freedom: *Nkosi Sikilel i Afrika!*[2] I know that today we are singing that hymn with tears in our eyes. We are singing it while we are bowed down by the weight of oppression and battered by the winds of injustice. We are singing it while our elderly languish in resettlement camps, and our children are dying of hunger in the "homelands." We are singing it now while we suffer under the brutality of apartheid, and while the blood of our children is calling to God from the streets of our nation.

We must, however, work for the day when we shall sing it as *free* black South Africans! We shall sing it on that day when our children will no longer be judged by the color of their skin but by the humanness of their character.[3] We shall sing it on that day when even here in this country, in Johannesburg and Cape Town, in Port Elizabeth and Durban, the sanctity of marriage and family life will be respected, and no law will sunder what God has joined together. We shall sing it on that day when in this rich land no child will die of hunger and no infant will die an untimely death; when our elderly will close their eyes in peace, and the wrinkled stomachs of our children will be filled with food just as their lives will be filled with meaning. We shall sing it when here, in South Africa, whites and blacks will have learned to love one another and work together in building a truly good and beautiful land.

With this faith we shall be able to give justice and peace their rightful place on the throne of our land. With this faith, we shall be able to see beyond the darkness of our present into the bright and glittering daylight of our future. With this faith we shall be able to speed the day when all South African children will embrace each other and sing with new meaning:

God bless Africa!
Guide her rulers!
Bless her children!
Give her peace!
O, give her peace!

Notes

Chapter 1

1. *The Cape Times,* Oct. 12, 1973.

2. Ben van Kaam, "Arbeid voor ongelovigen," *Je hoeft er niet geweest te zijn, Apartheid in de praktijk* (Baarn, 1973), p. 13.

3. Ibid., p. 8; emphasis added.

4. *Pro Veritate,* Feb. 1973.

5. See Rev. H. Snyders, *Die Kerkbode,* Dec. 16, 1970.

6. Adam Small, "Blackness vs. Nihilism," in *Essays on Black Theology,* M. Motlhabi, ed. (Johannesburg, 1972), pp. 14–15.

7. H. M. Kuitert, *De spelers en het spel* (Baarn: Ten Have, 5th ed., 1970), pp. 58-59.

8. Ibid., p. 52.

9. See James Cone, *A Black Theology of Liberation* (Philadelphia: Lippincott, 1970), pp. 203–27; Albert Cleage, Jr., *The Black Messiah* (New York: Sheed and Ward, 1969).

10. Van Kaam, "Arbeid," p. 11.

11. Beyers Naudé and Roelf Meyer, "Christusfees of Baalfees," an Appendix to *Pro Veritate,* Dec. 15, 1971.

12. F. T. Bakker wrote about this in *Gereformeerde Weekblad*, Oct. 12, 1973. Comparing an article by J. D. Vorster on "communal prayer," published in the South African periodical *Die Kerkbode* in 1973, Bakker concludes in his article that white South Africans continue to state the gospel in ideological terms just as M. C. Vos stated the gospel in ideological terms in the eighteenth century.

13. Cone, *A Black Theology*, p. 214.

14. J. Cardonnel, "Van konservatieve erfenis naar revolutionaire traditie," *Tijdschrift voor Theologie* (special number: *Religie van de toekomst, Toekomst der religie*), p. 116.

15. Ibid., p. 120.

Chapter 2

1. *Commentaries on the Twelve Minor Prophets,* Habakkuk 2:6, vol. 4, pp. 93–94; emphasis added.

Chapter 6

1. *Commentaries on the Twelve Minor Prophets,* Habakkuk 2:6, vol. 4, pp. 93–94; emphasis added.

Chapter 7

1. I became aware of this perspective in a conversation with Kosuke Koyama, from whose valuable insights I have profited very much.

Chapter 8

1. The *Sowetan* is a daily newspaper of the black township of Soweto (South West Township) on the edge of Johannesburg.

Chapter 9

1. P. Huet, *Het tot der zwarten in Transvaal mededeelingen omtrent slavernij en wreedheden in de zuidafrikaansche republiek* (Utrecht, 1869), pp. 29–30.
2. In Max Warren, *The Christian Mission* (London: SCM, 1951), p. 10.
3. For this insight I am dependent on Nicholas Wolterstorff, *Until Justice and Peace Embrace* (Grand Rapids: Eerdmans, 1983).
4. Quoted by W. Fred Graham, *The Constructive Revolutionary* (Richmond: John Knox, 1971), p. 70; emphasis added.
5. Ibid.
6. Quoted in Wolterstorff, *Until Justice and Peace Embrace,* p. 73.
7. Ibid., pp. 79–80.
8. Karl Barth, *Church Dogmatics*, II/I (Edinburgh: Clark, 1957), p. 386.
9. John Calvin, *Institutes of the Christian Religion* (Philadelphia: Westminster, 1960), IV, xx, 32, p. 1520.
10. Ibid., p. 1521.

11. Emphasis added.

12. Karl Barth, *The Knowledge of God and the Service of God according to the Teaching of the Reformation* (London: Hodder & Stoughton, 1938), pp. 227–28.

13. Wolterstorff, *Until Justice and Peace Embrace,* p. 21.

14. The thought expressed here is that of Chaplain General The Rev. Van Zyl of the Republic of South Africa.

15. Belgic Confession, art. 35; emphasis added.

Chapter 10

1. Statement by the black participants at the South African Council of Churches Consultation on Racism, Feb. 1980, published in the booklet under the same title (Johannesburg, 1980).

2. H. Gollwitzer, "Schwarze Theologie," *Evangelische Theologie*, Jan. 1974, pp. 45–46.

3. Francis Wilson, *Migrant Labour in South Africa* (Johannesburg, 1972), p. 189.

4. See D. P. Botha, *Church and Kingdom in South Africa.*

5. *Die Kerkbode*, Sept. 22, 1948, pp. 664–65.

6. Botha, *Church and Kingdom.*

7. *Institutes*, book 4, chap. 17, par. 38.

8. Statement by the black participants at the South African Council of Churches Consultation on Racism, Johannesburg, 1980.

9. *Gesammelte Schriften*, vol. 6 (Munich, 1974), pp. 350ff.

10. *Institutes*, book 4, chap. 20, par. 32.

Chapter 15

1. Cf. Martin Luther King, Jr., "I Have a Dream" address at the Lincoln Memorial, Aug. 28, 1963.

2. The National Anthem of black South Africans.

3. Cf. King, "I Have a Dream."

Other Orbis Books . . .

BOESAK, Allan
FAREWELL TO INNOCENCE
A Socio-Ethical Study on Black Theology
and Black Power

"Boesak provides a framework of review of current black consciousness, black power, black theology, and liberation theology and then offers a helpful, evolving black ethic. All the major black American and African theologians are included in summaries of these issues and are treated in adequate fashion. Boesak indicates his knowledge of the issues and in a brief concluding essay probes a black ethic that arises from oppressed peoples (e.g. black) and urges a reversal of much 20th century materialism 'to recapture what was sacred in the African community long before white people came—solidarity, respect for life, humanity, community.' " *Choice*

ISBN 0-88344-130-6 *197pp. Paper $6.95*

THE FINGER OF GOD
Sermons on Faith and
Socio-Political Responsibility
Foreword by Paul Lehmann

"Boesak is a South African student chaplain, and the excellent sermons collected here were written for his audience of young, liberated black Christians. Addressing hard political questions in a biblically centered fashion (scriptural passages introduce each sermon), Boesak more than meets his own criterion for good political preaching. Notes with background information on specific people and events will help American readers." *Library Journal*

ISBN 0-88344-135-7 *112pp. Paper $5.95*

ANSBRO, John J.
MARTIN LUTHER KING, JR.
The Making of a Mind

"Of the numerous books written on Martin Luther King, Jr., John Ansbro's will join the few enduring ones. Ansbro's major contribution is his focus on King's philosophical, theological, and moral development. In a carefully documented manner, Ansbro demonstrates the rich inner consistency and systematic character of King's thought." *Choice*

ISBN 0-88344-333-3 *368pp. Cloth $17.95*

CONE, James H.
FOR MY PEOPLE
Black Theology and the Black Church

"This is an important book for theologians of all ethnic persuasions. With his usual candor and self-examination, James Cone divulges some classified material on the difficult problem of relating Black theology—and liberation theologies generally—to mainline religious establishments." *Gayraud S. Wilmore, author of Black Religion and Black Radicalism*

"*For My People* is inspiring and educational. Dr. Cone's writing is scholarly, yet it can be understood and appreciated by ordinary people." *Richard Allen Hildebrand, Presiding Bishop, African Methodist Episcopal Church*

ISBN 0-88344-106-3 *288pp. Paper $9.95*

CONE, James H. & Gayraud S. Wilmore
BLACK THEOLOGY
A Documentary History

"It would be hard to imagine anyone talking or writing about Black theology without using this book as a reference. The six sections, each introduced by one of the editors, cover every aspect of the origin, development, and significance of a theological revolution in the United States which is still not clearly understood nor appreciated by the great majority of Protestants and Catholics. This is not only a documentary record but an eloquent and scholarly presentation of the issues and implications of Black theology. An extremely important book." *The Christian Ministry*

ISBN 0-88344-041-5 *672pp. Cloth $19.95*
ISBN 0-88344-042-3 *Paper $12.95*

DOBRIN, Arthur & Lyn, & Thomas Liotti
CONVICTIONS
Political Prisoners—Their Stories

"Dispassionate but compelling accounts of the experiences of individual political prisoners under a variety of authoritarian or totalitarian regimes in nine countries." *Fellowship*

"The nine vignettes describing the anguish of political prisoners that make up this volume are moving and in some instances unforgettable." *America*

ISBN 0-88344-089-X *128pp. Paper $5.95*

ERSKINE, Noel Leo
DECOLONIZING THEOLOGY
A Caribbean Perspective

"Erksine gives a picture, disturbing because it rings so true, of that 'colonial theology' which so often has legitimized the subjugation of the Caribbean's blacks. At the same time, he is critical of attempts to apply a merely American black theology or a merely Latin American liberation theology to people in a situation which has its own unique history and problems." *Bulletin of the Congregational Library*

ISBN 0-88344-087-3 *144pp. Paper $6.95*

EVANS, Robert & Alice
HUMAN RIGHTS
A Dialogue Between the First and Third Worlds

"This is the best volume on human rights for teaching that I have seen, and the one most provocative for the church's mission. The superb case studies and commentaries from around the world render it simultaneously global, ecumenical and concrete." *Larry Rasmussen, Wesley Theological Seminary*

ISBN 0-88344-194-2 *256pp. Paper $9.95*

HOPE, Marjorie & James Young
SOUTH AFRICAN CHURCHES IN A REVOLUTIONARY SITUATION

"A useful historical outline, from the first settlement of the Dutch East India Company in 1652, to the militant demonstrations by the Coloreds in 1980; a detailed *Who's Who* in the religious resistance to apartheid; brief but often frank and revealing interviews with a broad spectrum of church leaders and other activists. A modest but real contribution." *The Kirkus Reviews*

ISBN 0-88344-466-6 *282pp. Paper $9.95*

WALSHE, Peter
CHURCH VERSUS STATE IN SOUTH AFRICA
The Case of the Christian Institute

Dr. Walshe, a South African scholar and author long resident in the U.S., traces the development of the South African Christian Institute. It came as no surprise when the Institute, along with the remaining organizations of the black consciousness movement, was banned in 1977, having made a major contribution—and a lasting one—to the evolution of an indigenous liberation theology. This book, based not only on the ample documentary sources, but on personal interviews with all the leading participants, is likely to remain a definitive account of a short but immensely influential episode in modern South Africa's history.

ISBN 0-88344-097-0 *250pp. Cloth $19.95*

WILMORE, Gayraud S.
BLACK RELIGION AND BLACK RADICALISM
An Interpretation of the Religious History of Afro-American People

"The most important textbook on the history of black religion and the black church ever written. No student of black history and theology should be without it in his or her library." *James H. Cone*

"A landmark for all of us who seek both to understand and to transform the entire American experience." *Vincent Harding*

ISBN 0-88344-032-6 *320pp. Paper $9.95*